SEWARD HILTNER

is professor of pastoral theology in the Federated Theological Faculty of the University of Chicago and a widely recognized authority on counseling. Three of his other books in this field are described on the back of this jacket. He also writes for periodicals and serves as pastoral consultant to *Pastoral Psychology* magazine.

Dr. Hiltner spent the academic year 1958-59 in New Zealand, doing research and teaching on a Fulbright fellowship. In 1957 he served for four months as visiting professor in the Menninger School of Psychiatry, Topeka, Kansas.

THE CHRISTIAN SHEPHERD

THE
CHRISTIAN SHEPHERD
Some Aspects of Pastoral Care

SEWARD HILTNER

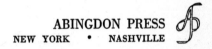

ABINGDON PRESS

NEW YORK • NASHVILLE

THE CHRISTIAN SHEPHERD: SOME ASPECTS OF PASTORAL CARE

Library of Congress Catalog Card Number: 59-7246

SET UP, PRINTED, AND BOUND BY THE
PARTHENON PRESS, AT NASHVILLE,
TENNESSEE, UNITED STATES OF AMERICA

to SIMON DONIGER

Conscientious and imaginative
editor of *Pastoral Psychology*

FOREWORD

The title of this book contains two metaphors. Jointly they suggest both its intent and its limitations.

"Shepherding" is our most ancient metaphor for the tender and solicitous concern that the church and its ministers are to exercise to all persons in need. The actual work of shepherding has been known more often as "pastoral care."

"Aspects" does not mean parts of, like slices of a pie, but perspectives on, like searchlights illuminating a single object. It suggests, on the one hand, that there is a unified object or theme—shepherding—around which all discussion centers. But it also connotes, on the other hand, that no particular number of perspectives or searchlights exhausts the meaning of the theme.

Thus the book has a single theme, shepherding or pastoral care, but it considers only specific modes or facets or aspects of that concern.

The original occasion for preparation of material that has resulted in this book was supplied by the Candler School of Theology of Emory University. The first four and the last two chapters have been developed from what I gave there as the A. J. Jarrell Lectures of 1957. Part of the same material—Chapters I, II, IV, and IX—served also as the Ida S. Wernicke Memorial Lectures for 1957 at Eden Theological Seminary. The substance of Chapters V through VIII constituted most of the Elliott Lectures for 1958 at Western Theological Seminary, Pittsburgh. I remember each of these occasions with warm appreciation to my principal hosts—to Dean William R. Cannon at Emory, to President Frederick W. Schroeder at Eden, and to President Clifford E. Barbour at Western.

In an earlier version, several of the chapters were also presented at schools and conferences for ministers in which I participated during 1957 and 1958—the Omaha School for Presbyterian Pastors, the Ministers' Retreat of the National Conference of the Church of the Brethren, two conferences under the auspices of the General Extension Division of Florida, one conference under the auspices of the University of Mississippi, and the Pennsylvania School for Presbyterian Pastors. The hospitality accorded me was memorable in each place—by Milo Bail at Omaha, by Stewart B. Kauffman on behalf of the Brethren, by Troy M. Wakefield in Florida, by William M. Jones, Jr., in Mississippi, and by Claude S. Conley in Pennsylvania.

The basic point of view represented in this book will be familiar to readers of my earlier books, *Pastoral Counseling, The Counselor in Counseling,* and *Preface to Pastoral Theology.* The novelty lies in the exploration of specific areas and dimensions of Christian shepherding about which I have not written before.

SEWARD HILTNER

CONTENTS

I. THE GOSPEL AND SHEPHERDING

Our age is witnessing a genuine and important revival of Christian theology. There is a new eagerness and a new energy at work attempting to delineate the Christian message critically and to hear and assimilate it religiously.

Biblical scholars, while continuing to advance the gains of technical study in linguistics, archaeology, oriental history, and textual criticism, are also approaching the basic religious meaning of the biblical message with new zest. Doctrinal or systematic theologians, while incorporating the gains of historical and philosophical scholarship, are speaking with new authority of the uniqueness of the Christian revelation. Christian historians, of Christianity and of other religions, although they have more scholarly precision than ever, are careful but convincing proclaimers of their faith. Christian ethics is taking on new stature and is helping to illuminate Christian faith as well as Christian life.

This critical exploration of the meaning of the faith for various dimensions of human life and learning is widespread. The arts and literature, psychology and psychiatry, the natural sciences, and other dimensions of learning are being examined, both to criticize their assumptions according to the insights of faith, and to determine the light they may shed on the meaning of the faith for our day. The theological revival is no withdrawal from culture and society, but neither is it a yielding to culture and society.

Whatever else this revival has done, it has certainly altered the theological dividing lines of a generation ago. Today we could say, with justice, that there is a new conservatism in Christian thought—a serious and critical attempt to save and to conserve what is basic and crucial in the unique Christian message, first in its biblical form and then in the reformation and rediscovery and outworking of that message by Protestantism. But we could say, with equal justice, that there is a new liberalism too—when liberalism is understood as the spirit insisting that the gospel be viewed in its full relevance to every need of man and society and to every achievement and failure of the human mind and spirit. The revival of our day insists at the same time upon the absolute uniqueness of the revelation of God in Jesus Christ, and upon the need to explore freely the precise relevance of this revelation to every dimension of our own day and time.

There are of course today, as in every age, real differences in interpreting the basic Christian message, and our emphasis on the common elements ought not to suggest lack of awareness of the differences. Some such statement as the following, although every Christian would insist on adding something to it and perhaps altering it a bit here and there, would appear to be increasingly acceptable.

The Christian revelation is unique, and it is the fact or event of Jesus Christ that makes it so. Jesus of Nazareth, who was fully man, came into history at a particular time and place. Jesus the Christ, the divine Son of God, testified to God's fatherhood of sinful man and wrought the means, once and for all, of man's redemption. It is this event of reconciliation that is final. No new type of work is needed by God in order to save man. But God, through the Holy Spirit, continues to work, that man may receive the revelation and be lifted from the sin and alienation into which he continually falls. Indeed something is required of man in accepting the good news of his salvation through Jesus Christ, but were it not for the grace that prepares man, even receptivity would not be possible. Thanks be to God in Jesus Christ who, by the might and the love of his Spirit, lifts us from isolation, bondage, and despair and makes us, unworthy as we are and continue to be, beloved sons and brothers in Christ. We are nourished in his Church, renewed by his Word, assured by the sacraments, and released through his salvation to give ourselves gladly, if still fallibly, in service, inquiry, and love.

It is some such message as this that we hear today from thoughtful and discerning Christians—granted all the variations made possible and even desirable by our justly cherished heritage of freedom. Uniqueness is proclaimed without obscurantism. Absolutely nothing can be regarded as of the same order as God's revelation of himself in Jesus Christ. But the nature of this revelation, and its reception in man's heart and mind, are not to be confused with a vague emotional loyalty, with a cold intellectual assent, nor with any other form of obscurantist defense by which man's sinful ego seeks to protect itself from the demands of the gospel.

Furthermore, such a core statement by no means answers all the questions. How is the gospel to be best communicated to men? How is it to be relevant to the affairs of society as well as to individual persons? How is this or that dimension of church life and activity to be as relevant as possible without compromise of the faith? Such questions require continuous attention and inquiry, as they have had throughout Christian history. The answers to them are not automatic, even to him who has most deeply received the gospel.

Gospel Basis of Shepherding

As a focal concept concerning ways of bringing the gospel to the particular needs of men in their problems and their sin, I have chosen to return to the ancient metaphor of shepherding. When this function is being performed, he who performs it is a Christian shepherd.

The terms that have been more common in the modern world—pastoral care, pastoral work, and pastoral counseling—are still of great importance, but the context from which they are drawn is a bit different from that of shepherding. I think of shepherding as a perspective. Any Christian shepherd, to some extent, has the shepherding perspective at all times. He is alert to the possible presence of particular need whenever or wherever it may emerge, but this will be his main or dominant way of viewing a situation only under some circumstances, not under all. Thus shepherding is always present as a readiness to emerge when called for by particular need, but it becomes the dominant factor in the situation only under particular circumstances.

Our whole inquiry is about Christian shepherding as one of the modes of outreach of the gospel to men in need. To be Christian, we must move from some such understanding of the faith as has already been suggested. To be relevant, we must study carefully and afresh the sense in which the roots and bases of shepherding are contained in the gospel itself. We need also to utilize any knowledge and wisdom we can get from any source—to the extent that it helps to clarify the meaning of the gospel, the nature of man's need, or the processes by which the riches of the gospel may be brought into revitalizing contact with that need.

As we have understood it, shepherding from the biblical

14

period to our own day is unique to Christianity. Other high religions have spiritual directors of one kind or another who deal with people as individuals or in small groups. But dealing with people in terms of shepherding, the essence of which looks toward healing in a holistic sense, is unique to Christianity and Judaism, and even in Judaism its development since biblical days has been quite different from that in Christianity.

The essential meaning and significance of shepherding, as it is unique in Christianity, is seen pre-eminently in the familiar story of the good Samaritan. We recall that Jesus used this story in reply to the lawyer's question, "Who is my neighbor?"

A man was going down from Jerusalem to Jericho, and he fell among robbers, who stripped him and beat him, and departed, leaving him half-dead. Now by chance a priest was going down that road; and when he saw him he passed by on the other side. So likewise a Levite, when he came to the place and saw him, passed by on the other side. But a Samaritan, as he journeyed, came to where he was; and when he saw him, he had compassion, and went to him and bound up his wounds, pouring on oil and wine; then he set him on his own beast and brought him to an inn, and took care of him. And the next day he took out two denarii and gave them to the innkeeper, saying, "Take care of him; and whatever more you spend, I will repay you when I come back." (Luke 10:30-35 R.S.V.)

Concluding his story Jesus asked the lawyer which of the three proved himself to be a neighbor. Even the lawyer had to reply, "The one who showed mercy on him."

This is, of course, a story with moral implications. One cannot profess one thing and do another. Every man is our neighbor. Good works are owed to every man in need. But the story says more than that. It implies that anything standing in the way of the best possible meeting of the need for healing is an offense against God. The priest and the Levite may well have been on their way to church. Nevertheless, Jesus' implied condemnation of them would not be lessened by any such possibilities. They were present. The testimony called for was healing. But they passed by on the other side. The unlikely Samaritan, on the other hand, despite the enmity between his people and the Jews, performed a healing service, as intelligently as possible under the circumstances. He manifested mercy and compassion in his attitude, and intelligence in his use of means.

Anything that should stand in the way of rendering the needed shepherding would be an offense against God, the story implies. Thus any gospel that is to be regarded as relevant to this situation must begin with shepherding. As we reflect on this, it becomes clear that we cannot grasp the deeper meaning of this parable without a consideration of timing. Perhaps the man going from Jerusalem to Jericho had made the trip a hundred times without incident. If the Samaritan had fallen in step with him on one of those occasions, he might well have presented verbal testimony to his faith. No oil or wine or bandages would have been required. But this time nothing else would do. What was needed was oil, wine, bandages, and an inn. This was the sole relevant testimony for this occasion. Whatever might be true in other places and at other times, the one way in which proper testimony might be given in this place at this time was by shepherding.

We may note further that the shepherding provided by the Samaritan on this occasion of need is not regarded in the parable as ancillary to something else. There is no suggestion that he got through this as an emergency in order that he might then move on to another order of function of more importance because it was "normal" in character. At this time, in the face of this need, shepherding was the thing. To put it in even sharper fashion, shepherding here was, for the time being, autonomous, requiring no justification from anything else.

The attitude revealed here, we are at once reminded, is like that of the shepherd devoting his energy and attention, at a particular time and place, to the one sheep that was lost, and temporarily diverting it from the ninety and nine who were not.[1] When the timing and need are of this kind, no other justification is needed. There is no counting of statistics. There is no plea of emergency against normalcy. Instead, there is attention according to need.

To the best of my historical knowledge, the basic attitude revealed in these stories is unique to Christianity when the full dimensions are considered. Other religions, of course, recommend good works arising out of faith. But only in Christianity is the effort to shepherd and to heal, when needed, regarded as *itself* the one indispensable way of communicating the gospel on those occasions.

To put the matter in more comprehensive terms, the way in which one testifies to the gospel cannot be determined in advance by the preferences of the testifier. Testimony must be given according to the need and condition, on any particular occasion.

One cannot say, "I have a single secure way of testifying to my faith on all occasions and do not have to take into account the relativities of human need." Instead, testimony to Christian faith is always a compound of the eternal gospel and specific need. Any attempt to wrap the gospel in a cello-

17

phane package, as if it could be given in the same way on all occasions, betrays what is required. The mode of testimony should be according to the need in the situation.

The great commission of Jesus to his apostles was "to preach and to heal," or "to preach and have authority to cast out demons." (Mark 3:14-15.) Both aspects of the commission are ways of presenting the gospel to the needs of men. They are not categorically different types of activity, nor do they have basically different aims. They are different ways of bringing what is absolutely needed to the hearts and minds of men, taking into account different situations, occasions, times, and needs. We should misunderstand the commission if we felt one aspect of it depends upon and is subsidiary to the other. Both preaching and healing are ways of linking the eternal gospel with specific need. Both are ways of performing the life-giving function. Neither, alone, is to be confused with the function itself.

Shepherding and Healing

It is the gospel command to heal that gives us the basis for the shepherding task. Lack of clarity at this point has often distorted the understanding of shepherding in the past.

The good Samaritan principle calls for the mode of testimony to be relevant to the nature of the particular need. When the need is for healing, then shepherding is called for. When the need is of a different character, then something else should be done that is not to be confused with shepherding.

Suppose that, in the good Samaritan story, it turned out that the robber's victim was really a member of the secret police intending, as soon as he recovered, to infiltrate the

Samaritan lines. Or suppose that the hundredth sheep, cared for so diligently by the shepherd when lost, should turn out to have a communicable disease against which the ninety and nine ought to be protected. In such situations other considerations than shepherding would become primary concerns, even though the need for healing would not be absent. We always hope that these various forms of interest will be united, and ideally they are. Curing the one sheep of his communicable disease is also the best protection for the ninety and nine. But we cannot assume that, in actual fact, these interests will always and automatically be in harmony.

Shepherding, therefore, does not describe the total function of the person we call a "pastor." He is also one who communicates the gospel and organizes the fellowship. Shepherding, communicating, and organizing—each of these provides a perspective from which all activities are examined. Each, under proper circumstances, becomes the principal concern. None should imperialize over the others. The ultimate goal of shepherding, like that of communicating and organizing, is to relate the gospel to the need and condition of men. Each is called on according to the nature of the need, not according to the subjective preferences of the one we call pastor.[2]

Rightly understood, all shepherding moves in the direction of healing even though circumstance may prevent actual healing or may prevent it at this time. This is to use the term "healing" in its general and comprehensive sense, involving the restoration of functional wholeness that has been impaired as to direction or timing. The aim of shepherding is to help the person (or the group smaller than the whole fellowship) to move as far in the direction of healing as circumstance permits.[3]

Jesus Christ, said the early interpretations of our faith, is the great shepherd.[4] We who have been called to be brothers of and joint heirs with Christ are to be undershepherds one to another.[5] We are members one of another in the body of Christ.[6] To be sure, we are imperfect and sinful members, but we are touched with his wholeness because we are organically interrelated in his body. To one another and to all men we are to act as shepherds, that is, as undershepherds, under the commission to preach and to heal.[7]

Despite the ambiguities that have often become attached to it, it is my conviction that the shepherding metaphor can be very powerful and useful to us. We do, however, need to purge it of possible wrong connotations. It grew out of a simple agrarian situation in which the shepherd took his flock by day out into the fields to graze, watched over them that they might not become lost or injured, protected them from enemies, and brought them at night to the safety of the fold. The Christian metaphor refers to the solicitous and tender and individualized care by the shepherd of the sheep. This is true whether the shepherd brought back a straying lamb with his crook or killed a wolf who threatened the flock. In the case of the straying lamb, the meaning of tender and solicitous concern in the shepherd does not prejudge the issue in favor of letting the lamb do anything he has a mind to do. If his straying in the interest of succulent morsels brings him too near a cliff, his recovery by the shepherd may appear to him to be judgment rather than love. If it is a person rather than a lamb, he will be consulted and not directed. Still, the experiencing of love or of judgment are both possible in shepherding.

When shepherding is so regarded, then it is clear that shepherding and healing, as defined above, are the same thing so far as aim is concerned. It is not that all shepherding can effect healing. Some shepherding has to be a matter of sustaining, of standing by, without power to bring about restoration, just as an injured sheep might die despite all the tender care of the shepherd or veterinary physician. But the aim is always healing.

Today we are so imbued with the great positive results that have emerged from modern scientific medicine, founded on differential diagnosis and treatment, that we tend to misunderstand the simple but profound conception of healing that is found in the New Testament. The New Testament intuitions are of a different order from that of differential diagnosis and treatment. We must separate them from such comparisons just as we do in connection with the physical world view of people living at that period.

The basic intuitions about healing in the New Testament seem to center around two points, one of which may be put negatively and the other positively. The negative point appears in connection with the concept of demons. The New Testament intuition was this: That which is central and crucial about the person, or the total spirit, is always larger and deeper than the negativities that may adhere to him. Whatever demons may be, they are not all of him. We see this, for example, in Jesus' story of the Gadarene who, precisely because he could say that his name was Legion, was bigger and deeper than the thousand demons at work within him.[8] Although we rightly reject a literal demonology, we note that the basic meaning of demons in relation to disease in the New Testament account was to distinguish the basic potential for oneness and integration and positive movement from the powerful and dynamic forces that threatened it and might even be, as with the Gadarene, for the time being in control.

Modern medicine and the related arts and sciences, in contrast to those of the previous century, are moving toward a similar idea.[9] Categorical distinctions between healing of body and mind seem no longer possible. There is abundant evidence that, even in those persons who are most sick or most impaired, there is energy working in the direction of health that transcends all conscious calculation—even though it does not by any means always succeed. Fortunately, we no longer talk about demons, but we do know that a dominating mother or a detached father, no less than a tubercle bacillus, may act just as the ancients thought demons did.

The other conviction or intuition of the New Testament about healing is seen positively—that real healing is of the "spirit," when spirit is understood to mean very much the same thing that we mean today when we speak of a whole person. A person may become ill or impaired at any level, all the way from the cells of his body to his relationship to God. True healing embraces all levels. There may indeed be differences among them, but the differences are not absolute and categorical.[10]

Increasingly the scientific evidence seems to point toward the possibility, certainly now far from realized, of a general and comprehensive theory of healing that will have relevance for cells and for the whole human spirit.[11] Some may be frightened by such a possibility, and indeed we ought to be frightened if what were envisaged were the reduction of the higher to the lower. If this were to be done by reducing "spirit" and "history" to "nature," then the Christian

22

intuitions would stand against it. I am referring to a different kind of healing. We now see that there is more of what has been called spirit and history within nature than has previously been recognized. This implies the opposite of reductionism.

Christians stand for the unity of the human person, for man as a total spirit including body, for men as members one of another, and for men as both sinful and at the same time, made in the image of God. If man is to be healed, all aspects or organs or relationships must be touched; whence it follows that each of these levels or orders or perspectives must somehow affect the others even though it need not by any means wholly determine them. It follows that our attempts to shepherd and to heal never exist in some walled-off compartment labeled "religious."

The more possible it is to think of healing in the inclusive sense suggested above, the plainer it will become that shepherding and healing are of a piece. It is often asked whether healing and salvation are the same thing, since their etymological history is so similar. The answer given depends in large part upon the specific meanings ascribed to the words and the context in which the question is seen. As the terms are ordinarily used, they come from different contexts, and therefore, issues can only be clouded by any appearance of equating them. But it may be that someday we too shall be able to ask, "Which is easier to say, 'Your sins are forgiven you,' or to say, 'Rise and walk'?" (Luke 5:23 R.S.V.)

II. BASIC PRINCIPLES OF SHEPHERDING

Our concern in this chapter will be to reach certain basic operating principles of Christian shepherding. As we have already noted, the place accorded to shepherding in Christianity is unique. It is not possible, however, simply to deduce all the operating principles from this fact. In order to advance our understanding, we need to examine actual shepherding situations. We shall do so in the light of our best theological understanding. We shall also look for any help we can get from such helping and healing arts and sciences as psychiatry, clinical psychology, and social work.

As actual shepherding situations have been studied in this way during recent years, it has become clear that some of the most basic things Christians have always believed about the process of shepherding are receiving strong reinforcement. Of all these convictions, the most important is that we cannot help a person in any real sense unless our interest in and concern for him are genuine. No matter how refined they may be, techniques alone, of any kind, will not be sufficient to help a person as a person. (They may of course help part of a person, or a person in some part of himself—as when a good bandaging job is done by someone we do not like.)

On the other hand, our modern studies have not confirmed all of our traditional notions of how to help or to shepherd. Some of our traditional practices have been found to be as wrong as was the medicine of an earlier day, when it tried to treat people by "bleeding" them. Thus we need to be

24

careful and discriminating, so that our basic convictions are not wrongly associated with poor methods by which shepherding is to be carried out.[1]

A Pastoral Call

As a starting point, we shall put before ourselves a fragment of an actual shepherding situation. We do this for several reasons. First, it will provide a concrete focus for our discussion; second, it will prevent what might otherwise seem to be an abstract discussion of principles, and third, it should help to insure communication, so that we know just what we are talking about at any time. We should note that this material is not merely illustration. It does not simply illuminate something we have found out in some other way. Used rightly, it demonstrates the very processes by which the principles were arrived at—granted that I did not reach them solely through examination of this specific situation.

This pastoral call was made by a minister we shall call Pastor Kell upon a woman who will be known as Mrs. Fry. Pastor Kell wrote up the call from memory immediately after it took place, which means that the actual call required probably two or three times as long as this necessarily abbreviated version will take in reproduced form. It is basically a simple type of shepherding situation, however—one of the sort that might happen to any pastor any day.

Mrs. Fry is in her thirties, is married and has several children, and has been for some days a patient in a general hospital. As the report itself will indicate, she is and has been a good Christian. Pastor Kell is not minister of Mrs. Fry's home church. At the time this call was made he was

25

studying under the direction of the hospital chaplain. As Mrs. Fry's pastor lived at a great distance from the hospital, Pastor Kell, who was a mature minister of experience and in his thirties, was assigned to see if Mrs. Fry required pastoral service. Prior to the present call upon her, Pastor Kell had made one brief call in which not much had taken place except greetings and, Pastor Kell hoped, some indication to Mrs. Fry that he was prepared to help if she so desired.

When Pastor Kell entered Mrs. Fry's room, he found her sitting on the side of her bed with her head lowered. Although she had invited him to come into the room after hearing his knock on the door, she had done so in a dreary voice. She looked low in spirit. Then the following took place:

PASTOR KELL: How are you this morning, Mrs. Fry? I decided to call on you again and see how you were getting along.

MRS. FRY: I am glad to see you. I am kind of down this morning. I don't feel that God has answered my prayers. I have prayed that I would get to go home today, and, you see, here I am. God has let me down, and I feel that I am forsaken. I think I'll just stop praying.

PASTOR KELL: You feel that God hasn't answered your prayer as you prayed, and that you have been let down?

MRS. FRY: Yes, I do feel that way. You remember Mrs. Smith, who was in the other bed there? Well, she got to go home. Then another woman was put in here with me, and now she's getting ready to go home. I'm able to get around more than they could, and my doctor keeps telling me that I can go home in a few more days. He keeps on saying that. I don't see why they were allowed to go home, and—here I am. (*She begins to cry.*)

PASTOR KELL: You feel that your doctors should let you go home,

26

and since your roommates have gone home—it makes you lonely?

MRS. FRY: I am better, and I can stay in bed at home. But I am so lonely here. Why did *they* get to go home, and I have to stay? I prayed so much, and I have had no answer. I might as well stop praying.

PASTOR KELL: I can see that your home calls you, and you would like to go to it. But I gather that God has answered your prayers on previous occasions?

MRS. FRY: Yes, I know he has. I have been so sick, and I prayed. Well, here I am, and better. I had so many things to go wrong with me. I wondered why those things came to me. I do not know what I have done for God to be punishing me. Why—?

PASTOR KELL: You fail to understand your suffering, but you know now that you are better? You have been given strength to bear, and believe that somehow God has a purpose in it?

MRS. FRY: Yes. I told my husband last night that it must be God's will for all of this sickness to come to me. God must have a purpose in letting me suffer. Sure, I know—I guess I am kind of down in spirit today.

PASTOR KELL: God has promised to help us. (*At this point he read the twenty-third psalm, Isa. 41:10, and Isa. 26:3.*)

MRS. FRY: That helps so much. Yes. (*She pauses and looks off into space.*) It is so hard to see through things sometimes. The doctor told me that I would have to be patient. Well, how can I after all these days here?

PASTOR KELL: "In your patience ye shall win your souls." The Word of God speaks to us. He says, "My grace is sufficient for you." God has been with you thus far, and I feel sure that you believe he will see you through.

MRS. FRY: Of course I believe that. I got so lonely when those other women went home. But since you came in and I could talk with you, I feel so much better. It is good to talk with someone about the things that bother you.

27

PASTOR KELL: It has been good to talk with you.

MRS. FRY: I wish you would come in again tomorrow. I would love to see and talk with you again. Thank you very much for coming to see me.

PASTOR KELL: I shall be back tomorrow. Good-bye.

As we move to discuss this pastoral call, it may be well to say that I regard it as ambiguous from the point of view of Pastor Kell's understanding of basic principles of shepherding. That is, it seems to me to contain some good things and some bad things and is neither a model to imitate nor a horrible example to avoid.

Concern and Acceptance

The first operating principle of shepherding that will be noted involves concern and acceptance. He who would be shepherd needs both to feel, and to express appropriately his own genuine concern for the person and his acceptance of the person as he is.

What this means in its simplest form is demonstrated right at the beginning of Pastor Kell's call. Immediately after the greetings, and with no further warm-up, Mrs. Fry said, "I don't feel that God has answered my prayers. I have prayed that I would get to go home today, and, you see, here I am. God has let me down, and I feel that I am forsaken. I think I'll just stop praying."

In saying this, Mrs. Fry knows perfectly well that she is addressing herself to a minister, who presumably believes in prayer and also believes that it is not God who lets people down. But she is not "baiting" Pastor Kell. This is no device that she has consciously contrived for a shrewd, political kind of testing. It is a test, to be sure, but one that

28

is given unconsciously, because it springs out of negative feelings so strong that they demand expression. The mood of Mrs. Fry's comment is one of reluctant defiance, but this feeling is expressed to one who plainly does not himself feel what she is feeling.

When we are confronted with an expression of feeling of this kind, the easiest, simplest, and most natural thing is to refuse to accept the feeling. Remember that the theme of Mrs. Fry's utterance has been "God has let me down." We would be tempted to say, "Really, Mrs. Fry, I hardly think God has let you down. The answers to prayer are not always what we expect." In terms of the theology of prayer, this is a correct comment; but to Mrs. Fry it would sound as if we were rejecting her by rejecting her right to have the feeling she has expressed. Without realizing it, we would be trying to "defend" God.

Or again, we might be tempted to say, "Well, I can certainly understand your desire to go home, but would it be wise for you to go home until the doctor believes you are ready?" This would avoid a head-on theological collision. But it would also evade dealing with Mrs. Fry's current negative feeling about prayer. It would shift the discussion, rather than coming to terms with the feeling.

Whatever his deficiencies at other points, at this one Pastor Kell resisted temptations of this kind. To the expression of Mrs. Fry's negative feeling he replied, "You feel that God hasn't answered your prayer as you prayed, and that you have been let down?" This assures Mrs. Fry that, so far as she has gone, Pastor Kell is prepared to accept the reality of her negative feelings. Since these are precisely the feelings that might make Pastor Kell reject her, the one way, at this stage, in which she can be accepted as a person is to have her negative feelings accepted.

Pastor Kell's acceptance of Mrs. Fry through accepting her right to have her feeling of reluctant defiance is not, be it noted, agreeing with her. He does not say, "I agree with you absolutely. God didn't answer your prayer so of course you should stop praying." Acceptance does not necessarily mean agreement. It means accepting the person through the one thing that makes it possible at the time, namely, accepting the very feeling that threatens the relationship.

There is a sense in which, theologically speaking, we should have known this all the time. Paul Tillich and other theologians of our day, in attempting to communicate to modern Christians what is the real meaning of the Protestant doctrine of justification through grace by faith, have presented this in terms of acceptance.[2] Through Jesus Christ, God accepts man, not in terms of his acceptability, but through faith brought about by the prevenient grace that makes faith possible. If man had to become acceptable in order to have God accept him, he would never make it.

Translated into shepherding terms, we could put the matter this way. If we had to get all our feelings to the point where the shepherd would wholly agree with them, either we should not need shepherding or we should be deceiving ourselves. If we operate as limited and fallible undershepherds in our ministry of help and healing, the crucial test is always what we do in relation to that which is unacceptable. If we, representing the Great Shepherd, can accept only that which is acceptable (what we agree with), then we certainly communicate to the person in need the idea that he must become wholly acceptable before God in Christ will accept him. Such a conclusion is mistaken theologically and psychologically. Theologically it will lead him to new and frantic attempts at works of merit in order to become acceptable. Psychologically it will lead him to "repress," as Freud terms it, all negative feelings out of his awareness.[3] The feelings will still be there operating within and upon him, but they will be less accessible and therefore more difficult to change.

Here is a striking instance in which psychological and theological understanding reinforce each other to give the clue to a basic aspect of shepherding. Without acceptance there is either repression or fruitless striving. Without acceptance of the feeling that is negative, there is no acceptance of the person who holds it. Without acceptance of the person, with all his conflicts, negativities, defiance, misinformation, and sin, no Christian shepherding is taking place. Acceptance, then, is crucial. Theology and psychology combine at this point to give clues on how to effect it.

The fact is, however, that no amount of technique will enable us to be genuinely accepting in the sense described here, unless we have a genuine concern for the person we are trying to shepherd. Now, at this moment, absolutely nothing is permitted to stand in the way of our feeling of concern for this person. Even if the person, like Mrs. Fry, is angry at God for what we know to be mistaken reasons, we are concentrating on this person—not, for the moment, upon God, prayer, our being a minister, or anything else. This is precisely like the story of the lost sheep, or that of the good Samaritan. Right now, the occasion being what it is, this is the exclusive focus of our conscious concern, from which we will not be diverted. At other times and on other occasions, we may indeed concentrate our overt attention upon God, upon prayer, and upon other matters. But here and

31

now, to be genuinely concerned for Mrs. Fry means that nothing is permitted to divert us from concentration on her, her concerns, and her feelings.

The first principle of shepherding, then, is accepting the person as a person through accepting his feelings—crucially this means that aspect of his feelings that is negative. In order to do this, we have to give undivided and concentrated attention to that person as he is. This is made possible by following through the implications of as genuine and disciplined a concern as our fallible flesh is heir to. Thank God that we never have to have unconditional concern and acceptance, for we humans are not capable of that! We can, however, do something to cultivate it in sufficient measure to manifest the genuineness both of our concern and of our acceptance.

We have dealt so far with concern and acceptance in their simplest forms. They are often more complex. For example, in the latter part of Pastor Kell's call upon Mrs. Fry, there was a point at which she said, "The doctor told me that I would have to be patient. Well, how can I after all these days here?" Up to this point, Pastor Kell had reasonably well accepted the negative, as well as the positive, side of Mrs. Fry's feelings as she had expressed them. The positive feelings had begun to emerge, as they usually do, once the negative ones have been accepted. Mrs. Fry had said, "God must have a purpose in letting me suffer." This may or may not be good theology, but it indicates a new and genuine resolution on her part to accept her condition. Had Pastor Kell followed his own general approach to acceptance, he would have been undisturbed to see the negative feelings reappearing. But apparently this bothered him. So he quoted some scripture and concluded, "God has been with you thus far, and I feel sure that you believe he will see you through."

In the actual pastoral call, it is not clear that this altered approach by Pastor Kell did any serious harm. Mrs. Fry at once admitted that what Pastor Kell had said was true. But here is the difficulty. She will, because she has had these negative feelings before and because she is fallibly human, have them again. Suppose she gets the impression from Pastor Kell that he is willing to accept her first negative feelings until the positive feelings begin to emerge; but that, he having done his duty, from then on she should have no more negative feelings. When he said, "I feel sure that you believe he will see you through," did Mrs. Fry say to herself, "Of course I had those feelings, and he was so accepting of them; so obviously I cannot have them again"? Pastor Kell did not intend this, but it is possible that this is what he produced.

The communication to people of our genuine acceptance of them, especially when there has been much rejection in their lives, is seldom done in one well-chosen phrase or in one pastoral call. Sometimes this is a long and trying business. I recall a brilliant woman in her fifties with whom I had a dozen or more pastoral interviews some time ago. She had had some severe experiences of rejection in her life; and, in spite of my best efforts, she found it difficult to believe that I really accepted her. Since her reaction to non-acceptance tended to be one of hostility, and since I am fallible, the fact was that I was often below my own standard of acceptance. One day she came to my office and simply blew up at me. With great insight and shrewdness she ticked off what was wrong with me. This was by no means water rolling off a duck's back for me. I had come to have a genuine concern for her, and I felt we had been getting somewhere. Besides, I had to admit to myself that about three fourths of her denunciations were right, or at least right enough to make sense. Finally, when I had a chance, I admitted this fact. That closed the interview. On the next occasion it became clear that something very positive had happened. She said, "When you could take me almost at my worst, I finally felt that you were accepting me as I am." Although situations of this kind are bound to be uncomfortable, they may at times be necessary if acceptance is to be a reality and is itself to be accepted.

Concern and acceptance are of course closely akin to love and understanding. They simply represent different aspects of the same phenomena. We humans are always incapable of agape in the full Christian sense; but nowhere more than in shepherding is there need to approach this as closely as we can. Perhaps genuine concern, a more modest word, is more useful to us since it implies our concentration on the other person without demanding of us an unattainable perfection. The more genuine our concern, the greater the chance that we may be vehicles for transmitting agape.

Similarly, understanding is like acceptance. It is the specific process by which our will to accept may be implemented, first in our own feelings, and then in communication to him we would help. Pastor Kell could not accept Mrs. Fry as a whole and ignore or reject her feeling of defiance. The grasp of what is to be accepted—indeed, of that which is most difficult to accept—is the function of understanding. Seen in this light, love and understanding necessarily go hand in hand with concern and acceptance.

34

Clarification and Judgment

The second basic principle of Christian shepherding involves what we shall call "clarification" and "judgment." As we have already seen, most genuine shepherding begins when there is expression of negative feeling, which is then, in considerable measure, accepted rather than rejected by the shepherd. We have also noted that the expression and acceptance of such negative feeling ordinarily results in the emergence of some positive feeling. We must now deal more carefully with this latter point.

What usually happens is not the clear emergence of positive feelings so that the negative feelings cease to exist, but instead the emergence of both types of feeling together. About midway through the pastoral call on Mrs. Fry, Pastor Kell had concluded a comment by saying, "But I gather God has answered your prayers on previous occasions?" To which Mrs. Fry replied, "Yes, I know he has. I have been so sick, and I prayed. Well, here I am, and better. I had so many things to go wrong with me. I wondered why those things came to me. I do not know what I have done for God to be punishing me. Why?"

In noting that she had prayed to get better, and then *had* got better, Mrs. Fry is expressing an emerging positive feeling, but it does not stand alone. It is still ensconced in a dominantly negative feeling context: Is God punishing her? Why did so many things go wrong with her? Why all this time and suffering? What do we do at such a point as this? It is no longer merely a question of accepting negative feelings. There are two types of feelings, and what do we do with them?

From the previous discussion, it is surely clear that we

cannot effectively ride the positive feeling and ignore or reject the negative. By the same token, we cannot now concentrate entirely on the negative feeling as if the emergent positive feeling were to be distrusted. What we need to do is to acknowledge and accept both types of feeling—which means accepting, understanding, articulating, and clarifying the fact that a conflict exists between the two feelings.

Here is what Pastor Kell said at this point, "You fail to understand your suffering, but you know now that you are better? You have been given strength to bear, and believe that somehow God has a purpose in it?" Perhaps it might have been done more effectively. Still Pastor Kell succeeds in lifting up, stating, clarifying, in other words, the two forces that are in conflict within Mrs. Fry's feelings, in so far as she has revealed their nature to him. It is not a generalized statement indicating that she is in conflict; for what she needs to do is to deal with the two feelings openly and directly in their specific nature. But as she becomes able to do so, it is also borne in upon her that a conflict does exist. The ability to recognize that a conflict exists, and that in some measure we grasp its nature, already indicates that she, her uniquely human selfhood, is in some way bigger than the conflict. To put it in theological terms, the ability to confront real conflict is itself proof that one is a finitely free and self-transcendent creature and not merely a victim. It is no accident that the idea of "crisis" is now prominent in both psychiatry and theology.

Psychologically speaking, clarification is the process by which forces that have been shadowy, vague, and therefore unassailable, are brought into the arena of awareness where they can confront each other in daylight and fight it out. As Freud noted, this is not possible so long as the antagonists are on different levels. Anxiety has prevented the two forces from an encounter. When genuine acceptance in the shepherding relationship has helped to diminish the anxiety, then the forces may emerge and be ready for clarification.

It is important for us to recognize that we cannot tell in advance what kinds of feelings may be most difficult for this or that person to bring to the arena of clarification. Some may find it most difficult, as did many of Freud's patients, to bring unacceptable sexual impulses into the open. Others may discover, as do so many psychiatrists today, that feelings of hostility lie most deeply buried. On the other hand, I have dealt with people who would far more easily acknowledge impuses to rape and murder than they would admit hidden desires for tenderness or gentleness or for being less than self-sufficient. This is why clarification can never be done merely in general, or just in principle, but always, if it is to be effective, must be done in terms of the specific conflicting feelings.

We have noted that, theologically speaking, the person who can clarify conflicting feelings is already demonstrating to himself that he transcends the conflict in a way that he had not previously dared to hope. This does not mean that all will solve itself automatically, but it does mean that, if there is a battle of values, it can be fought out on its own terms.

The great temptation of the shepherd, when conflicting feelings begin to come into the open, is to ride one side at the expense of the other. Recall the point at which Mrs. Fry began to articulate both positive and negative feelings at the same time. How easy it would have been for Pastor Kell to fall into the trap of saying, "I realize you've had a bad time; but you do admit that you prayed to God to get well, and here you are better, don't you?" At once Mrs. Fry would have had to feel guilty for still harboring the negative side of her feelings. Trying to keep them out, then, she would have failed to get them into the light of day, where they could engage in real encounter with the more positive feelings.

As a matter of fact, I believe that in a subtle way, and contrary to his conscious intention, Pastor Kell did do something like this to Mrs. Fry toward the close of his call upon her. He moved too quickly and too eagerly to read the reassuring passages of scripture. He told her, in effect, that her positive feelings were more real to her than the negative. He failed to help her clarify the fact that she would, in all probability, continue to have a conflict between positive and negative feelings—between faith and doubt. Reading the scripture was not wrong, but he should have laid a foundation for reading it. It should not have been used in such a way as to increase her sense of guilt at having negative feelings. Nevertheless, the virtues of Pastor Kell's call certainly outweigh the mistakes.

Clarification in the psychological sense seems very close indeed to what we mean by judgment in the Christian sense. When shepherding is needed, and we remember that this is not on all occasions, it is more than likely that the person is overwhelmed by shadowy negative feelings. Like Mrs. Fry, he may set these feelings forth defiantly, but the very defiance reveals his dissatisfaction at having them. That is, his self-administered judgment is largely negative.

Since our aim in such a situation involves altering that negative self-judgment to a more discriminating grasp of forces both positive and negative, it is sometimes said in psychological circles that counseling and psychological therapy should eliminate all elements of judgment. If judgment is thought of as words or evaluations from outside, imposed on the person, it is true that we want to eliminate it. Such external judgments, we know full well, will simply result in a heightening of defenses, making the conflict and the problem less accessible.

By judgment in the Christian sense we mean something quite different. We mean something that comes from within rather than something imposed from without, and we mean good news of release rather than bad news. Take, for instance, the idea of "conviction of sin." In the true Christian sense, he who is convicted of sin has received good news, not bad. He knows that without the assurance of forgiveness beyond any merit of his he could never have accepted the fact that he was convicted. The conviction, then, is a process moving from within, but made possible by a potential release that is far above and beyond his own doing. Thus the judgment, inwardly accepted, is already an indication of release. As many Christians have said, only the redeemed man can know the enormity of sin. The man still in bondage cannot afford to admit the depth of his sin. In the language of judgment, the redemptive character of God's judgment can be felt only by the man who has, in some measure, received the reality of God's love. Judgment of any other kind is not Christian but is an escape from the claims of God in Christ.

Clarification, then, leads to the potentiality for experiencing judgment in the Christian sense, internally and as good news, for it betokens something beyond itself. What often happens is something like this. A person indicates to us that he has some kind of problem. As he sees it, this is troublesome but only partial; it does not touch his whole self. As he begins to deal with it in an atmosphere of genuine acceptance, he finds that the problem was deeper and more pervasive than he had originally thought. At the same time more of the elements of the problem or conflict are able to be brought to the light of day; hence it becomes more possible of solution. Until there is recognition of the breadth and depth of the problem, there is little hope of solution. But until the elements are brought up for clarification, there is little chance of seeing how pervasive the problem is. What seems to happen is that a new hope, dim and vague, comes first, brought by grace. This enables more judgment to be assimilated. That in turn makes possible the acceptance of more that is positive, until finally the judgment is seen and felt as necessary, and ultimately as good news.

With judgment as with clarification, our pastoral temptation is to ride one side at the expense of the other. Often we do this by moving prematurely to the supposedly positive elements, as if we could bypass the process by which the judgment is slowly turned from negative to positive. With the person of deep inferiority feelings, we are likely to point out all his good and strong points—thus making it less possible than ever for him to get the inferiority feelings into the open for clarifying. We often find that beneath a person's inferiority feelings he has concealed and exaggerated notions of his own importance. The one way in which shepherding can deal satisfactorily with judgment is for us to have patience and to be willing to stand by with the person while the painful clarifying process is taking place. Any misguided notions of sympathy on our part that result in premature reassurance (of which Pastor Kell was partly guilty) run grave risks of turning the person aside.

Conclusion

Time has permitted our dealing with only two of the basic principles of shepherding—first, with concern and acceptance (linked with love and understanding); and second, with clarification and judgment. We have attempted to study these in a concrete situation in order to shed light on them, both psychologically and theologically.

By this type of exploration it is hoped that we have also gained some insight into the meaning of theology itself at certain points, especially concerning the actual process by which man's redemption through Jesus Christ takes place.

The discussion might have extended also to a third basic principle of shepherding, namely, the specific ways by which the shepherd may reflect upon his own part in the shepherding activity and may thus bring more humility and self-understanding to his task.[4]

There are many ways in which the principles of Christian shepherding may be organized, studied, and discussed. I believe the mode followed in this chapter is as basic as any other—especially because it throws into relief some of the ways in which modern psychology and Christian theology may be supplementary in our understanding and executing the shepherding task.

III. SHEPHERDING GRIEF AND LOSS

The shepherding of persons in situations of grief and bereavement is almost the sole problem area in which the church and the pastor still exercise a virtual monopoly. Pastor and church have much to do with marital problems, parent-child problems, problems of loneliness or anxiety, and many others; but in relation to these, new experts have arisen—physicians, clinical psychologists, social workers. Their work may be a great resource to church and pastor. Indeed, a growing number of them inform their work as well as their personal lives with Christian commitment, so that there is no neat division of a Christian pastor on one side and secular helpers on the other. Nevertheless, when it comes to grief and bereavement, this above all else is regarded as the function and prerogative of the pastor.

The Shepherding of Mrs. Henshaw

How can Christian shepherding best operate in times of grief and bereavement? We shall set forth an actual situation in which a young minister attempted to mediate help on such an occasion. Let it be stated unequivocally that this really happened and is faithfully reported. And let the reader be warned that this pastoral call is ambiguous and is not simply a horrible example as it may at first appear. This call was made some years ago, when the man we shall call Pastor Barton was just beginning his study of shepherding. Since then he has become an excellent Christian shepherd.

At the time this action took place, Pastor Barton had been only four weeks in a new pastorate. Because he was completing a semester in theological school at the same time, he had made almost no pastoral calls during that month of settling. One evening, on arriving home, he found the news waiting that Mr. Henshaw, about fifty years of age and in apparently good health, had just been stricken dead at his dinner table. That same evening Pastor Barton made a brief call upon Mrs. Henshaw and her fourteen-year-old son. Arrangements were made for the funeral service, and simple expressions of sympathy were offered.

After conducting the funeral service two or three days later, Pastor Barton spoke briefly to Mrs. Henshaw. For some reason that Pastor Barton forgot to put on paper when submitting his work for criticism, and which I have since forgotten, he did not make a subsequent call upon Mrs. Henshaw until three weeks after her husband's death. No doubt most of us would feel that that was a mistake on Pastor Barton's part regardless of the circumstances. But let us note that point and get on with the story.

When Pastor Barton did arrive at the Henshaw house, three weeks after the death of the husband and father, he found Mrs. Henshaw in her kitchen engaged in cooking. Her mother was present; and, turning the cooking over to her, Mrs. Henshaw led Pastor Barton to the living room. Pastor Barton selected what he called a "comfortable overstuffed chair," and Mrs. Henshaw sat in another on the opposite side of the reading table. These were the respective chairs, the pastor surmised, in which husband and wife had ordinarily sat. Until they sat down, the pastor reported that there were the usual greetings and pleasantries. But then, on being seated, Mrs. Henshaw was silent; and so, for a full minute, was Pastor Barton. Then the following took place:

PASTOR BARTON: How are things going now?

MRS. HENSHAW: Very much better now. I am beginning to get our business affairs all straight. There is a persistent emptiness to life, but I must expect that until I take up some kind of work.

PASTOR BARTON: Have you anything in mind?

MRS. HENSHAW: Yes, several things (*There was a half-minute pause while she was evidently thinking, but as she said nothing and the pastor did not wish to seem to be prying, he spoke*).

PASTOR BARTON: I really came here for a purpose this afternoon.

MRS. HENSHAW: Yes, I could tell by your manner.

PASTOR BARTON: And you must suspect that I intend to talk about death. (*Mrs. Henshaw made no reply, but was absorbed in thinking.*)

PASTOR BARTON: Sometimes I have to speak to people much less frankly than I shall to you. Your religious background and your considerable education have determined me to speak very frankly about the greatest danger in time of bereavement—that of falsely identifying self-pity as grief. (*Pausing for a few seconds*) Sam is gone from your life now. But he is beyond pain—nothing more can happen to cause him unhappiness or misery. We assume that he is happy now; at least we assume that he is beyond unhappiness. His life in the flesh is ended, and he lived a full, happy, and satisfactory life.

MRS. HENSHAW: (*Pensively*) Oh yes, he often said to me that he wished I could get as much satisfaction out of life as he did. (*Pausing*) He got so much satisfaction out of giving things to people (*again pausing*).

PASTOR BARTON: So now his life here with you is ended, and you cannot add to nor take away from it. Thus I want to tell you that all your thoughts about him must be self-analyzed the moment they begin to cause you what is commonly called "grief."

Scrutinize your thoughts for any element of self-pity. Say to yourself, "Am I sad because Sam is dead? Or because I am doomed to live out the rest of my life without him? Or because I have the sole responsibility of guiding and counseling our son?" Then if you find elements of self-pity, terminate them at once and force yourself to breathe a prayer of gratitude that your life with him was so beautiful and that he lived so complete a life in so short a time.

MRS. HENSHAW: Yes, I know that danger. But I have never faced it quite so honestly. (*With a light smile, wholly good-humored.*) You operate with a sharp knife, doctor.

PASTOR BARTON: Truth is a two-edged sword, madam (*banteringly*). You can even beat about the bush with such a sword and eventually destroy the bush. (*Pausing*) But I knew you would rather face it directly.

MRS. HENSHAW: It is better in the long run. (*At this point she paused; then a light suddenly suffused her face.*) They keep telling me I should live for my son now. You have never said that to me.

PASTOR BARTON: I think that will be your first great mistake if you do it. But you aren't going to, are you?

MRS. HENSHAW: (*Almost defiantly*) No!

PASTOR BARTON: You tell me why you won't, and then I'll tell you why you shouldn't.

MRS. HENSHAW: Because he has his own life to live, and I have encouraged him to do so since he was eleven years old.

PASTOR BARTON: Exactly. He is in high school now. You intend that he shall go to college. Being a normal boy and very personable, he will have many friends and will probably marry early. Then you would have to begin your life alone definitely. But you would be four or maybe six or eight years older. It will be much easier now to begin standing on your own feet. Offer the boy wholesome companionship rather than an overdose of mothering in an attempt to make up for the fathering he won't get.

MRS. HENSHAW: That expresses almost what is in my own mind. He's such a wholesome boy. (*She pauses for several seconds.*) Tell me, Mr. Barton, why do I sometimes get confused about the meaning of life? The day seems complete—the year—so much of nature seems complete. A caterpillar completes one cycle and becomes a butterfly. But we never seem to complete anything. No matter what we do in life, there is always something else to do, something more to accomplish. Why isn't the cycle of our lives ever complete? Why can't we actually complete one thing before we have to go on to something else?

PASTOR BARTON: Wait. Would we ever really complete anything? Is it human nature to be satisfied with any state of being that can be maintained over a period of time? No, our feelings of satisfaction are only fleeting; then we go on to new attainments. This chapter of your life is ended. You must now start a new chapter—or even a new book—with a new theme, a new plot, and a new setting.

MRS. HENSHAW: Yes, I know that, and I can do it. I worked before I was married, you know, and I have financial security for years ahead. But it is going to take a little while to get over the emptiness. (*After a considerable pause.*) You know, I want to tell you again how very deeply I appreciated the way in which you conducted the funeral service. You know that Sam's parents and his sister are all devout Roman Catholics. They were disturbed when he left that church to marry me, and I had been afraid they might make some unpleasantness at the funeral service. But they didn't, and I think this was mainly because of the dignity and good taste of the service itself.

PASTOR BARTON: Of course I'm very pleased that you felt that way about the service.

After several minutes of additional discussion like the last recorded, Pastor Barton arose to leave. Mrs. Henshaw thanked him sincerely for his visit:

Mrs. Henshaw: You have given me new purpose and courage. (*Then as Pastor Barton went down the steps, Mrs. Henshaw called out to him.*) And if I find myself weakening, I'll feel free to phone you to come to see me and bring that sword along.

Before proceeding to an evaluation of this pastoral call, I want to confess candidly that I have regarded it as a classic ever since the young pastor submitted it to me for criticism several years ago. Although this is the first time I have written up my reflections upon it, I have drawn upon it in a number of classes and in pastors' conferences and believe I now have a rather good guess as to what the pastoral reader's evaluation of it is likely to be.

In the first place, and most obviously, Pastor Barton walks with heavy shoes. Or, to change the metaphor, he acts for the most part like a pastoral bulldozer. Let us list a partial catalogue of his obvious errors without bothering to elaborate the plain reasons why they are errors. He makes the initial assumption that Mrs. Henshaw's problem is likely to be self-pity, without ever trying to draw her out as to what her problem and her feelings really are. He then sprays her with his diagnosis. He implies, even states, that feelings of grief are wrong and urges Mrs. Henshaw to force them out or terminate them. In the fact of happiness in Sam's life he sees a silver lining for Mrs. Henshaw, which he proceeds to sew into her cloud.

He uses bantering humor at a time and in a way that seems inappropriate to us. He uses a quiz show technique in dealing with her feelings about her son, first telling her what they ought to be. He gets her thinking ahead to the eventual marriage of her now fourteen-year-old boy, and adjures her not to overdo the mothering. When Mrs. Henshaw finally has a chance to talk on her own, she expresses beautifully and wistfully the eternal question of life's incompleteness. Pastor Barton, braver than Plato or Saint Paul, tells her in four choice sentences that her question is not relevant and that human beings are always dissatisfied. He concludes by implying that she should put everything of the old life behind her, forget it, and get on with the new.

In the face of this apparently blunt, forceful, immature, insensitive, non-listening comedy of errors, is there anything that can be said *for* Pastor Barton? Here we must ask ourselves the really basic question: How is it that, amid all the errors Pastor Barton made, his call seemed to be genuinely helpful to Mrs. Henshaw? This cannot be answered by saying that she was merely being polite to him. For this you must perhaps take my word. Knowing Pastor Barton, as well as studying his report and discussing it with him, I am fully convinced that Mrs. Henshaw meant every word she said to him about the positive value of his call. This makes the question more poignant: How, with all the wrong attitudes and methods, did he, nevertheless, accomplish good?

The answer lies, I believe, in a subtle combination of forces, characters, and circumstances related to the process of grieving. Let us examine initially the beginning of the call. The pastor and Mrs. Henshaw have sat down, and there is silence. Then in response to a general question, Mrs. Henshaw comments on the empty feeling she has, but becomes practical by indicating that she intends to get a job. The pastor follows this, but she does not wish to discuss it in detail. Then the pastor plunges directly into the discussion of grief. Mrs. Henshaw had apparently sensed his intention even before he spoke.

We have already expressed regret that he acted like a bulldozer, assuming that Mrs. Henshaw's grief problem was one of self-pity and giving her no chance to indicate how she did feel. On the other hand, he had and demonstrated the courage, despite the youth, inexperience, and immaturity of which he was not wholly unaware, to talk directly about death, and to call it d-e-a-t-h and not various euphemisms like "passing away." However we may criticize *what* Pastor Barton said and the way he said it, all this seemed to be received as quite secondary by Mrs. Henshaw. What she took as primary was the integrity and courage of this inexperienced young man, who cut through all the sentimental hemmings and hawings about death and went right to the point.

During the early days of World War II, before this country was officially engaged, gasoline rationing was instituted. The men brought to Washington to administer this, like those in many other emergency programs, were still feeling their way. One day it was announced that Protestant ministers would receive ration A stickers, while Roman Catholic priests would be entitled to B, or more generous rations. The reason given for the discrepancy was that the priest performed specific religious functions when he called on people, while the Protestant minister simply engaged in social visiting. This was not the result of plotting on the part of the Roman hierarchy. Besides, the Protestant churches succeeded in having the rations equalized at once. What is significant is that the new and inexperienced Washington officials reflected the common-sense view of the

American people that Protestant ministers simply do social visiting with their people.

There is a great temptation for the American minister to pussyfoot about something like grief. The motives are impeccably humane—be sympathetic, considerate, gentle. People have had a severe shock, and we do not want to add to it. The result is often that, on the one hand, people believe we are afraid of death and of grief; and, on the other hand, we miss great opportunities to foster the grieving process in the proper way.

Inexperienced and inept as he was, Pastor Barton was nevertheless willing to risk whatever emotion Mrs. Henshaw might show when the death was directly mentioned. I believe this courage communicated itself to Mrs. Henshaw, and that she saw beyond the blundering method to the courageous heart. In the further blunderings, which we have already catalogued, I believe Mrs. Henshaw continued to see beneath the surface and the content, and accepted Pastor Barton in terms of his spiritual intention.

In drawing this conclusion, however, we have already implied another, namely, that Mrs. Henshaw was herself a person of great spiritual strength. Many persons, both men and women, would simply have gone to pieces under the impact of this pastor's sledge-hammer blows. That Mrs. Henshaw not only did not do so, but also was able to see beneath the surface crudity to the honest intention below, is proof of the genuineness of her spiritual strength. Pastor Barton, we may well say, was lucky to have tried this on Mrs. Henshaw rather than on many others.

Our understanding of the grieving process has been greatly aided by the research on this subject carried on for more than a dozen years at the Massachusetts General Hospital in Boston. Since a number of people, including myself, have written about this research, only a very brief summary of the findings will be given here.[1]

Perhaps first in importance is the new meaning given to the great beatitude, "Blessed are those who mourn for they shall be comforted" (Matt. 5:4 R.S.V.). In its original sense, being comforted means being "with courage" or "with fortitude." The fact is that those who are able to mourn or grieve will also become capable of being with courage, and that, conversely, those who are not able to mourn or to grieve will not be with courage. In more prosaic terms, the grieving process cannot be bypassed with impunity. It requires spiritual strength to be able to mourn.

The grieving process, or the "grief work," as the Boston researchers have called it, may take many legitimate forms with different people. But in all of them there must be painful recollection of the deceased person, with an increasing capacity to "tolerate" the "image" rather than a compulsion to avoid the image or to repress everything into the unconscious. The "emptiness" that Mrs. Henshaw described is not something to be got over as rapidly as possible. Indeed, her capacity to feel this was an indication that the earliest stages of the grieving process had been successfully negotiated. She was then rendering accurately the continuing inner feeling that she had. If she could not have acknowledged it, it would have caused further trouble. We conclude that Mrs. Henshaw had a remarkable capacity to confront the suffering of her husband's death right from the beginning; and three weeks later had already entered upon a second phase of the process. That she was not afraid to confront the reality of her feeling, and that she could make tentative steps toward the future, are further indications of this fact.

We must make a final point about Pastor Barton and Mrs. Henshaw. If she had gone so far in working through the painful grief, even at such an early stage, and was thus demonstrated to have unusual spiritual strength; and if Pastor Barton was so inexperienced and inept as he proved to be—then what *could* this pastor have had to bring to Mrs. Henshaw in her bereavement that she did not already have? This question is vitally important for every young pastor who is honest enough to admit that many of his parishioners have a spiritual maturity he does not possess. And it may not be irrelevant to the pastor of any age.

The answer is that even the most inexperienced young pastor may have something to bring to someone of the spiritual maturity of Mrs. Henshaw. So far as we can see, this spiritual strength in Mrs. Henshaw was genuine. But the more genuine it was, the greater the likelihood that the feeling of emptiness and lostness, while diminishing, will continue for a long time, and that she will have periods in which emotion wells up from within, and she simply feels for a time like weeping, or going to bed, or sitting idly, or mentally reviewing the last days with her husband. *We* know, and the young minister should know, that such actions are not backslidings or "weakenings," as Mrs. Henshaw called them in her final remark. Instead, they are signs of the healthy movement of the painful process of grieving.

Mrs. Henshaw, because she lives in a culture that is afraid of death and the emotion connected with it, does *not* know this. She came thus far in her own grieving with a strength we may all envy. But she does not understand what is strength and what is weakness. If she finds herself, three weeks or three months later, breaking into sobs, she will diagnose this as weakness, when in fact it will be strength. If she gets herself a job prematurely, trying to "occupy her mind" (as no doubt many of her friends will suggest) before the grieving process is far enough along, she may regard this as a mark of strength, whereas it may be in fact weakness if done too soon. Well-intentioned friends may commend her for all kinds of apparent strength that is in fact weakness. On this, her pastor, however young, can be of help—provided he understands the full implications of the fact that comfort comes only through mourning.

As an appendix to the case of Mrs. Henshaw, one may of course ask: Why did the pastor not make use of any of the distinctively Christian resources in his ministry here? I would agree with the thrust of this criticism, but let us be certain we criticize the right thing. Surely it would have been no better than the actual situation had Pastor Barton made his call, read from the Bible, and offered a prayer, with no attempt to individualize his shepherding—especially by listening—to Mrs. Henshaw. Had these things followed the proper listening, they would indeed have been in order.

Beyond this, a reader may ask, what about the nature of the Christian hope in the "resurrection of the body" rather than in the "immortality of the soul," as the New Testament scholars have recently reminded us? Should he not have conveyed to Mrs. Henshaw something of the depth and reality of this Christian hope? Again I would agree, provided this should come *after* he had listened sensitively to her. But this Christian hope, however intepreted, cannot be an insurance policy against the suffering of grieving. The Boston research has records of persons who attempted to use Christian belief in a future life as a cushion against the suffering of grieving, to the detriment even of their physical condition.[2] The essence of the Christian hope is that God will save that which is worth saving, somehow, and that this has to do with us as whole beings and not as disembodied ghosts. What this means, no man knows. The essential faith is central to the Christian message. To attempt to use it as a defense against the suffering of grief is something quite different.

Loss

Grief for a deceased person who has been loved is so obviously final and stark that we sometimes fail to note the similarities it has with other forms of loss experience in life. We tend to be paternalistically indulgent, for instance, about broken ''puppy love.'' We had it once, we say to ourselves, and got over it; in fact, it did us good. What would life have been like if we *had* married that girl? But in so saying, we are completely forgetting the poignancy that accompanied the experience. We have allowed our culture to distort our recollection, and hence to make us less sensitive to the continuing poignancy of this sort that we may encounter.

Loss can assume many forms. While ordinarily far less deep and intense than grief, the essential process that must be followed in order to deal with it, however, is the same. One needs to learn to live with the image of that which is lost, rather than repressing it; and that means a more or less painful process of learning to tolerate the image. The difficulty comes very often in that we are guided by well-intentioned but mistaken people, who have in turn been misled as to what is going on, to try to deal with the loss by denying that it is a loss. That is, we are indirectly taught to be dishonest with ourselves about our own feelings.

Here is a man of middle age, highly successful in his occupation. For fifteen years he has done able work in the same job for his company. The job, the associations, the struggles and activities, all these are like old friends to him. They wear the garb of beloved familiarity. One day the company's president calls him into his office, tells him how much his work has been appreciated, and, over a pair of Corona Coronas, indicates that he is to be promoted to vice-president in charge of the office on the West Coast. There is to be more money, more recognition, and more of various things. Plainly this is a promotion. Our man is elated, but after his wife has received the good news that evening, he begins to muse over an unread evening paper. The prospect of leaving job, friends, all that is familiar, begins to rise in his mind. Steadfastly he pushes it away, "One simply cannot refuse such an offer. What a silly reaction to have!" So he goes on to the promotion, inwardly troubled for a very long time, not because he is incapable of making new friends and new familiarities in new surroundings, but because he regards it as silly to grieve for the old.

There can be no doubt that some of the older people who pull up stakes in Keokuk or Kalamazoo, and go to Florida or California, find something very positive in their move. But there is among not a few of them a good deal of un-grieved grief over what they have lost. When the perora-tions about the wonders of climate become too frequent and artificially cheerful, one wonders if a few tears shed for

Keokuk snow might not enable the sunshine to take care of itself for a day or two?

This tendency to try to handle loss by not admitting that it is loss seems considerably accentuated by the peculiarly American view that eyes must always be kept on the future rather than on the past. That this has a positive side goes without saying. But it has also negative consequences. As the scientist who is unfamiliar with past discoveries is unlikely to make new discoveries, so the assimilation of the future benefice is unlikely unless one is coming to terms with that which is of the past and is now lost.

When viewing loss in this light, I am convinced that it needs far more attention than we have even thought of giving to it. It is time that our shepherding took loss seriously, according to its inner meaning to the persons involved. If the loss process, like that of grieving, can be helped, encouraged, and carried through, then there *is* release for the future, for new experience, for new achievement. If, on the other hand, loss cannot even be felt as loss, then the negative consequences spill over into all kinds of apparently unrelated emotional symptoms, senses of meaninglessness, and anxieties.

IV. SHEPHERDING THE FAMILY

The object of shepherding is persons, but not monads. The notion of the person as an isolated unit, enclosed by mental, as well as physiological skin, cannot possibly be sustained. We become human and remain human because of our relationships.[1] These relationships are not external, to be understood merely as part of environment. They are the very stuff of which our selfhood is made. Those we love and those we hate are part—an essential and not an accidental part—of our selfhood.

Of all the social relationships that enter into the creating and sustaining of the form of our selfhood, those of the family are the earliest and the most powerful. It is an exaggeration to say that a child's character is so fully formed by the age of five or six that no real change can be made in it thereafter. At the same time, we have new respect for the profundity with which early family relationships mold character for good or for ill, and of the consequent difficulty in making basic alterations when that influence has been ill. Studies of babies whose physical needs are well met, but who have been deprived of the warmth and affection of a mother or mothering person, have been shocking in showing a stunting of development at all levels including the physical, even to the point, in some instances, of death itself.[2] If any new evidence had been required to show the basic and internal importance of the family for all that is essential to the development of the person, we now have it in abundance.

Now comes the paradox. At the same time that we have masses of new evidence that proper family nurture is absolutely essential to the development of selfhood, we have equal masses of new evidence that no family can produce the goods, or produce them all the time. The more obvious forms of family imperfection are so well known to us that they deserve no more than mention here—separation and divorce, drunkenness and infidelity, cruelty and callousness, quarreling and indifference. The subtler forms of family imperfection, however, can be no less devastating.

Here, for instance, is a pair of "good" parents with whom I talked recently. Not only are they people of fine character, they are good Christians and active church members, with sensitive social consciences and real capacities for warm and affectionate relationships with other people. From the time their boy was born eight years ago, their every thought was toward his being given all the love and security they knew a baby requires. Now, eight years later, confronting a real crisis in the life of the child, the mother said to me, "I realize now that I was so anxious to give Billy love that what he often felt was the anxiety instead of security, and this has now made him incapable of asserting any normal independence."

It is all too easy to say of such a situation: "That couple should have known better than to work at it so hard and so anxiously. If they had just relaxed, everything would have been better." Perhaps, but let us look at a family in which warmth and affection were given without working at it hard and anxiously. These are also good parents in all possible respects, and they are more competent than the couple described above. The individuality of their children is accepted and encouraged. Because the children were

58

helped to feel secure, they learned how to assert their own independence and also how to accept needed discipline without confusing it with rejection. Here is son Bobby, now twelve. He is smart, well-adjusted, properly independent but well related to other children and adults, physically and athletically co-ordinated for his age, and many other positive things. He is what most American parents hope their children will be at his age. But there is another side to Bobby. He has no inner comprehension of nor sympathy for others who lack his qualities. In dealing with the boy in his class who is crippled as a result of polio, he is the soul of courtesy. But he has manifested almost sadistic cruelty, as harmful as it was unintended, to another schoolmate who was deeply disturbed over the divorce of his parents and who desperately needed a friend. Without giving further illustrations, we may summarize by saying that his courteous but smug self-containment puts him well on the way to "success" as an adolescent and adult, but it is likely to prevent him from having any real capacity to accept the fact of the world's agony, either in Hungary, in the Middle East, or in his next-door neighbor. Quite literally, he will become the teen-ager who is never bothered with pimples or a touch of acne.

This insistence on interpreting paragon Bobby as ambiguous may appear arbitrary. "After all," someone may object, "he is only twelve, and there's plenty of time for him to learn those desirable human sympathies of which you speak. Haven't his parents done a remarkable job of rearing him so far, and aren't they likely to continue this in the desirable direction?" To be sure, nothing in human development is a closed issue; and certainly the parents have done an outstanding job, which they are likely to continue. But how, we may ask, could the parents have lived sensitively in a world of sin, war, crime, and heartbreak and yet have completely insulated themselves and their family circle from these realities? Have they brought up Bobby by a form of "inner-worldly asceticism," in which the family has been encapsulated against contact with all those realities that Christians have asserted are the essence of the "world"? Have the parents never felt and acknowledged tumult in their own souls? Have the world's sin and evil never got to them? If not, the Christian diagnosis is not that they are sinless but that their pride has prevented even the first step toward repentance. In psychological language, their defenses are intelligent, so intelligent that they work practically all the time, but at the price of a certain lack of human sympathy in themselves and the children they rear.

This story and its purpose should not be misunderstood. Parents are not being advised to return to authoritarian methods of child rearing. It is not recommended that stories of war and crime be placed temptingly before children. The point of the story is that even the best family is ambiguous. The more effectively it tries to be a good family, the more subtle become the ways in which the negative results emerge. We ought indeed to try for the best possible positive consequences, but let precisely that family that thinks it stands take heed lest it fall.[3]

Changing Attitudes

Not long ago I came across a most perceptive analysis of changing attitudes toward infancy made by Martha Wolfenstein. This is made by examining the successive editions of the booklet *Infant Care*, first published by the

U. S. Children's Bureau in 1914. Most of the comparisons and contrasts are made between the 1914 and the 1942 editions. The attitudes expressed at the time of the respective years of publication, Wolfenstein rightly suggests, tend to represent the majority opinion of specialists at the time. The attitude of the general public tends to lag somewhat behind this. In general, I should hazard the guess that the views expressed in the 1914 booklet came to dominate public opinion in the 1920's, while those expressed in the edition of 1942 came to represent majority public opinion in the 1950's.

Here are some excerpts from Martha Wolfenstein's discussion:

The conception of the child's basic impulses has undergone an extreme transformation from 1914 to 1942. At the earlier date, the infant appeared to be endowed with strong and dangerous impulses. These were notably autoerotic, masturbatory, and thumb-sucking. The child is described as "rebelling fiercely" if these impulses are interfered with. The impulses "easily grow beyond control" and are harmful in the extreme: "children are sometimes wrecked for life." . . . The mother must be ceaselessly vigilant; she must wage a relentless battle against the child's sinful nature . . . for thumb-sucking, "the sleeve may be pinned or sewed down over the fingers of the offending hand for several days and nights," or a patent cuff may be used which holds the elbow stiff.

In contrast to this we find in 1942-45 that the baby has been transformed into almost complete harmlessness. The intense and concentrated impulses of the past have disappeared. Drives toward erotic pleasure . . . have become weak and incidental. Instead, we find impulses of a much more diffuse and moderate character. The baby is interested in exploring his world. If he happens to

61

put his thumb in his mouth or to touch his genitals, these are merely incidents, and unimportant ones at that, in his over-all exploratory progress.

In the early period there is a clear-cut distinction between what the baby "needs," his legitimate requirements . . . and what the baby "wants." . . . This is illustrated . . . in the question of whether to pick the baby up when he cries. In 1914 it was essential to determine whether he really needed something or whether he only wanted something. Crying is listed as a bad habit. . . . "After the baby's needs have been fully satisfied, he should be put down and allowed to cry." . . . In 1942-45 wants and needs are explicitly equated. "A baby sometimes cries because he wants a little extra attention under some circumstances just as he sometimes needs a little extra food and water." . . . What the baby wants for pleasure has thus become as legitimate a demand as what he needs for his physical well-being. . . .

In 1914, playing with the baby was regarded as dangerous; it produced unwholesome pleasure and ruined the baby's nerves. . . . In the recent period, play becomes associated with harmless and healthful motor and exploratory activities. . . . Play is now to be fused with all the activities of life. . . . It is now not adequate for the mother to perform efficiently the necessary routine for her baby; she must also see that these are fun for both of them. . . . Play, having ceased to be wicked, now becomes a new duty. . . .

The conception of parenthood has altered. In the earlier period the mother's character was one of strong moral devotion. There were frequent references to her "self-control," "wisdom," "strength," "persistence," and "unlimited patience." . . . In the most recent period parenthood becomes a major source of enjoyment for both parents (the father having come much more into the picture than he was earlier). The parents are promised that having children will keep them together, keep them young, and give them fun and happiness.[4]

Let it not be thought that at any point the Children's Bureau was expressing extreme opinions. For such an extreme, we may turn briefly to a passage from John B. Watson's *Psychological Care of Infant and Child:*

Certainly a mother, when necessary, ought to leave her child for a long enough period for over-conditioning to die down. If you haven't a nurse and cannot leave the child, put it out in the backyard a large part of the day. Build a fence around the yard so that you are sure no harm can come to it. Do this from the time it is born. When the child can crawl, give it a sandpile and be sure to dig some small holes in the yard so it has to crawl in and out of them. Let it learn to overcome difficulties almost from the moment of birth. The child should learn to conquer difficulties away from your watchful eye. No child should get commendation and notice and petting every time it does something it ought to be doing anyway. If your heart is too tender and you must watch the child, make yourself a peephole so that you can see it without being seen, or use a periscope.[5]

Amid the humorous excitement engendered by this excursion into the recent past of our own attitudes, it is hoped that the point being illustrated will not be forgotten. This point is certainly not a cynical suggestion that opinions vary from time to time and one is as good as another. On the contrary, the views of the later period have much solid evidence to support them, or at least most aspects of them. Nor is the main point for our purposes specifically about babies and attitudes toward them. Our point is rather about the ambiguities in even the best family or the best attitudes in family life. Attitudes toward babies are easier to examine than attitudes toward older children, but the essential thing is the underlying view of family attitude toward its own function with any of its members.

From the perspective of today, it is hard not to laugh at the duty-centered mother of 1914, determinedly keeping in check all her own warm impulses to cuddle and play with her baby except when she can justify these activities by obvious needs for nutrition and cleanliness We may feel pity as well as humor in relation to the little father of 1914 who simply was not there.

But how much more difficult, and necessary, it is to get a proper perspective upon the attitudes of our own day! For instance, I would contend that the positive values of self-demand feeding of babies—the baby is permitted to eat whenever he wants to eat until he establishes a schedule of his own—are well established, work greatly to the benefit of the baby, and after the initial rough period for the parents are no more difficult than an imposed schedule.

What happens when the mother's anxiety to do the right thing prevents the baby from getting on to a schedule or from eating the minimum suggested by the doctor? The answer is that her anxiety increases. The principle upon which she operates may indeed be superior, but her anxiety may contain more ambiguity for the baby than did the moralistic authoritarianism of the mother of 1914.

To use one more brief illustration, a generation or a half-century ago it was not uncommon for successful fathers to put on a good deal of pressure that their sons might follow in their own occupation. In terms of direct pressure, or apart from sheer economic necessity, this has now become rare. It is regarded as bad form, and as fairly sure to make the teen-ager lose affection for his father. What we now find is a more diffuse and generalized ambition on

father's part—namely, to let his boy be anything he likes
so long as he is successful at it. In its capacity to produce
anxiety, this can be both more subtle and more devastating
than the old form of parental ambition.

Perhaps this point about the ambiguity of the family in
performing its basic functions appears to be overstressed.
It may be so. For there are many positive factors in the
American family situation at the present time that this
account has not mentioned. But at least as a corrective, an
account like the present one seems greatly needed. Even
a good deal of the discussion of family in Christian circles
seems far more intimately related to what Martha Wolfenstein calls the "fun-morality" of the family than with the
recognition of ambiguity in even the best Christian family
life.

The Christian Family

Our concern is of course with shepherding the family.
But our analysis and illustrations of changing attitudes toward and within the family have been necessary in order
to reach the question: *What* family? Very shortly we shall
get on to the *how* of family shepherding. But unless our
minds are thoroughly disabused of the notion that only the
divided, quarreling, or emotion-ridden family is in need of
Christian shepherding, the discussion of *how* will do little
good.

Our theology should already have told us that *every* family, and not just the "bad" or "neurotic" family, needs
shepherding at some times. Quite briefly, we may review
the Christian and Protestant bases for this statement.

Five basic assertions may be made about the family and

65

its function, upon which all Christians, including Protestants, agree in principle.

First, the family is a part of the natural order of life established by God and therefore inherently good. Second, the family is to serve both personal and social needs. It is to help the individual to *become* according to his best potentiality, and it is to see that the nature of the becoming is socially acceptable and responsible. Third, the family is to be monogamous, not so much for reasons of sex alone, as in order to protect the needed bases of loyalty between the spouses and between parents and children. Fourth, although there may indeed be a functional division of labor between the sexes, in the sight of God they are equal. In Christ there is no male or female. Finally, the family is to be regarded as the basic educational unit of society, and, in the performance of this function conscientiously, is not to be interfered with or superseded by any other social institution. On these principles all Christians would seem to be agreed.

These are by no means the sole principles held by Protestants in interpreting the function and meaning of the family. Let us look briefly at the principles especially emphasized by Protestant Christians. The first arises from the doctrine of the universal priesthood of believers. This doctrine is not merely a denial of the need for any priestly intermediaries between God and man. It is also an assertion of every man's direct relationship to God, on the one hand; and on the other hand, of the need for every man to be and to become, as needed, a priest to his fellow. From this doctrine it must follow that even the family cannot usurp the function of the individual person in his relationship to God; and that the intimacy and closeness of family ties provide unusual opportunity and obligation for each, on occasion, to be priest to the others.

Second, Protestants emphasize the availability of God's grace—the freeness of grace, as against the notion of its being earned. For the family this means that even the "good" family could not possibly be good enough. Its very "goodness" would be negated by its pride, smugness, and self-satisfaction. By implication the more truly "good" family, regardless of its specific situation and problems, would be the family steadily repenting of its sins in such a way as to be open to grace unmerited. It would be characterized by its attitude and direction rather than by its achievements.

Third, Protestants emphasize the universal need for regeneration and for justification and assert that these come by grace through faith, not works—that works of merit are a result and not a cause. Like the individual person, no family is above the need for regeneration. The family in obvious trouble may know this fact more securely than the "good" family, aware of everything except its sin of smugness. Both types of families move through crises and problems, with more or less success. Both need to recognize the need for regeneration in every crisis, and then to accept the grace that can provide the motivation for solution. The grace may indeed need to be implemented by technical means, but without an attitude of reliance upon it, regeneration not only cannot take place but is felt to be irrelevant.

Fourth, Protestants stress the absolute sovereignty of God. The historic battles over this and related issues between Calvinists and Arminians should not be allowed to obscure the basic agreement, that God alone is Lord and sovereign judge over all—and that therefore no person, or group, or institution can assert or erect anything that is not subject to that lordship and that judgment. In the latter form, Paul Tillich has called this "the Protestant principle." For the family this implies, not only that no existing family can be regarded as above judgment, but also that our best notions of the "ideal family" are equally to be put under God's judgment. The ideal as well as the actual family may be idolatrous. Not infrequently it may require far more spiritual discernment and humility to put the ideal family under judgment than the actual family. The family, like the individual, may acknowledge its existing troubles but insist on preserving the illusion that it knows precisely what it ought to become. From our Protestant principle, any such conviction must be under constant judgment, criticism, and examination.

Finally, among the principles we shall note is the Protestant conception of the church as being in some basic way a fellowship of those God has called and who have heard that call, as against the church's being regarded essentially as a visible institution. There is a voluntary principle. In most of Protestantism, this is felt to involve something about man's will to receptivity as well as God's free election. Applied to the family, there must also be a voluntary principle; the commitment of each to each, and each to all, cannot be forced. Further, the visible family, either actual or ideal, is insufficient as a guide to family development unless it partakes in repentance and humility of the whole family of God.

Shepherding Families

Any minister's count of the types of problems that require his shepherding attention would show marriage problems in first place. Put more accurately, it would show that the "presented problem" has to do more often with marriage than with anything else. We now know with fair certainty that there are very few marriage problems that were not, and are not still, first individual and personal problems. The necessary intimacies of the family have precipitated them perhaps as never before. But as they did not originate entirely in this family relationship, a direct attempt at reparation of the family relationship may be insufficient to solve them.

A great number of the situations in which marriage is the presented problem are brought to us by one person. Frequently this is the person who, by any ordinary standards, is more sinned against than sinning. For example, ministers are approached by the spouses more often than by the alcoholics themselves; and the same tends to be true when the threat to the marriage is sex, cruelty, irresponsibility, or detachment. Most of it, whatever it is, is likely to be in the partner who does not seek out the pastor.

It is not a new saying, but still an important one, that in these situations our shepherding needs first to be with those who are accessible to us. Perhaps later it may, and should, include other members of the family. Be that as it may, much can be done with the person who *is* ready for help. Take, for instance, the wife of a man who has become a genuine addict to alcohol. She is not responsible for this pattern in the sense in which her husband is, and yet only rarely has she failed, quite unintentionally, to contribute to the network of causes that has produced the pattern. Even if on a statistical basis she had been only one per cent responsible for the condition, new insight into that part might yet make an enormous difference in relation to her husband.

More important, with the alcoholic pattern now set, it may or may not be possible for her husband to be rehabilitated. If so, she may need to learn new ways of understanding her husband, or new means of avoiding provocation to alcohol. If not, she must learn how to live for herself, her children, and mankind. Whatever the marriage problem, and whatever the problem of her husband and its chance of solution, she herself has a problem the solution of which is as vital to her family as it is to her own integrity.

What the pastor is tempted to do in such situations is to assign degrees of blame, and then try to deal with the one who seems most guilty or with the couple together. Rigid rules are not possible, and there may indeed be situations in which this is appropriate. But even in those instances, I would contend that a mistake is being made unless, first, the person who has asked for help is given some help in terms of the situation as his or her own personal problem. When this is done, the *how* is not basically different from any other shepherding. It would follow the basic principles outlined in our second chapter.

There are, however, many family situations in which I believe direct help can be given to a couple together.[6] These can be handled in such a way that, if the help that can be given in this fashion is inadequate, the groundwork is laid for the more extensive individual help that may be required. In brief summary, here is a situation of this kind.

Sue telephoned to ask if I would be willing to consult her and her husband, Bill, about some problems in their marriage and family life. Sue said she was the one who had first felt some outside help was needed, but that Bill was quite willing to come. This turned out to be correct. Still on the telephone, I told Sue that I would be glad to talk with them (and made a date to do so), but that in the first meeting we would reconnoiter and decide what could and could not be done in joint discussion.

Bill and Sue appeared, and after the usual greetings, I made a speech before they were asked to tell their story. This was, I hasten to add, a short speech, but a speech nevertheless. It presented briefly my philosophy of help on family problems. If personal and intrapsychic problems of depth and long standing were involved, our concentrating on the marriage and the relationship within it would be insufficient. It was important that this be understood in advance. On the other hand, if the main problem really was the marriage relationship, even though there might be individual problems too, then a brief series of sessions might help. Following the present contact, I asked if each of them would be willing to see me separately, and have the three of us meet together for a final session. They agreed. I repeated that by the time of the final session it might be clear to either or both of them that they would profit from further individual counseling of some kind.

My rationale for this initial procedure should be fairly plain. In a brief series of interviews with two people, it is simply not possible for either or both of them to do concentrated work on their own inner issues or conflicts. Had I let them proceed at once to a statement, or statements, of the issue in the family situation, the assumption they would have made would have been one of two types: either that, at the end, I would render a series of pronouncements to them; or that I would proceed precisely as in working with an individual. Neither would be possible. Hence the importance of defining explicitly what might or might not be accomplished. If this procedure actually could help the marriage situation, fine; then the warnings about need for personal counsel could be forgotten. If not, then groundwork for needed help would have been laid from the first word.

In this first joint interview, Bill and Sue took turns telling the story, the gist of which was that each felt a general incompatibility with the other. Although well educated, Bill had taken a "start at the bottom" job in the conviction (with which I agreed when he explained it in detail to me later) that this would be best in the long run. Sue, however, felt Bill was lacking in ambition. He had been promising her for a year that he would soon be promoted, but this had not happened, and Bill did not seem to Sue to be concerned about it.

On the other side, Bill felt Sue was too sloppy about the house and in taking care of the children. He was all for her outside-the-home interests, he said, because he thought they were necessary to her happiness. But he did not see why, on coming home every afternoon, he had to lift a tricycle out of the front hall and see dishes stacked in the sink. Sue said she certainly was not a German *Hausfrau* but that she got her work done and kept the children happy. Yes, said Bill, she fussed so much over the children that he could hardly ever get them to do anything with him.

So it proceeded; and for our purposes, that is a sufficient sample of the actual content. I encouraged each of them to talk about himself, and about his feelings in relation to the other. Near the conclusion of our hour-and-a-half conference, the initial ground had been covered rather well. I attempted to make a summary restatement, using words and phrases each of them had used, of Bill's feeling toward Bill, of Bill's feeling toward Sue, of Sue's feeling toward Sue, and of Sue's feeling toward Bill. I indicated that in the individual contacts with each of them that were to follow I would ask them to correct me and expand, so that when the three of us met for a final session, we could see whether this rather direct method of getting at feelings and attitudes could prove sufficient to get something of a new direction going. I said that I promised nothing and had no more idea than they did whether this would turn the trick.

The interviews with Bill and Sue individually moved with unusual speed into areas of considerable depth. Spontaneously, each went into the family background both of himself and of the other, in accounting for certain current feelings. But the bulk of attention was on the present situation. At the conclusion of each of these individual interviews, I again summarized the feeling and attitude of the one toward himself and toward the other, and *vice versa.*

When the three of us met for what had been agreed on as the final session, I began the interview by summarizing what had taken place to date. I then invited them, with no further specific suggestions, to take it up. They did so, hesitantly at first, beginning with lesser things. It was plain that the depth achieved in the individual interviews was not to be brought out lightly where it might disclose the vulnerability of one's armor. But each, it soon appeared, had been thinking both of the other and of himself in some new ways. Sue said she saw, for instance, what Bill meant when he said that timing of the promotion did not really matter, and that she also saw what her impatience and general highstrungness did to distort when they confronted a situation like this. Bill heard this with approval, although it was obvious that he would have to see it work in action for a while before he would really believe Sue had seen the light.

Sue's reaction was similar when Bill indicated he had been looking at the dishes and the tricycle in a new way, and realized that he had been reading some of his mother's modes of housekeeping into the very different person and situation of Sue. And so it went.

At the end, I summarized and went a step further in indicating the broad pattern of irritation of each by the other that had emerged. The steps in the irritation process were different on both sides, but they had appeared in so many situations that I could speak of them as general patterns. At the close I again indicated that I still did not know whether this would enable them to turn the corner in their marriage. If not, personal counseling for one or both would be necessary. If so, thank God, and please report honestly back to me. At the end of two reports and one year of elapsed time, things were far from perfect, but tolerable and very much better. The same things were still irritating to each; but the step-by-step process from initial irritation to final outbreak was being frequently arrested in mid-course by both.

One may indeed say that the shepherd here was fortunate, and I agree. But the real point of this story is not that, as I defined the limited goal, it was successful. It is that, whether it had worked or not, I believe there is little likelihood that it would have done harm. There was some indication that, even if unsuccessful, it would have greatly facilitated having either or both of these spouses move to get personal counseling as it might be needed. If this last were not true, I would regard the procedure as too risky even for experimentation. Even so, I would not attempt this unless I felt some indication of basic stability in both the spouses. On those occasions when circumstance has forced me to talk with husband and wife together, when I have had only a negative intuition about basic stability, I have felt the over-all situation was not improved and sometimes worsened by the discussion.

The situations described up to this point still involve problems felt specifically as problems by families in rather obvious forms of distress. What about the "good" families who feel none of this but who yet, by our Christian diagnosis, are more subtly in need of shepherding? The answer lies mainly in what is done publicly in order to stimulate the expression of need privately. If we should ask a group of ministers whether they have ever preached a sermon on such topics as the following, I wonder what the reply would be: "What the Good Family Doesn't Have"; "People Are More Important Than the Family"; "Is There a Christian Way to Rear Children?" Perhaps we would be pleasantly surprised. Weekday evening meetings might well discuss the Christian family, drawing on material such as has been indicated here. Shepherding requires more than a pastor's intention; it also implies a parishioner's receptivity and acknowledged sense of need. For the fruition of this we may indeed have to wait on the work of the Holy Spirit. But presentation and discussion in sermons and other ways may help.

There is one other way in which needed shepherding may be fostered with "good" families. This is by readiness to hear seriously what people say to us either in casual contacts or in contacts where the focus is on something else. On such occasions we are likely to have our minds on anything except the persons. For instance, here is a member of the official board, a genuine pillar of the church, with good sense, energy, and a sense of humor. In moving out of a board meeting one night he said to the pastor, "I'd better get along; my wife said to be home at nine o'clock, or else." Our pastoral impulse is to joke, or to tell about *our* wife, or both. But just suppose, without his quite realizing it, that Mr. Pillar is really in trouble—that something quite important is masked behind this unconscious testing of the pastor's receptivity. If the pastor is alert, he does no harm to the cause of humor by saying, "Do you really mean a little of that, or are you just joking?" I find, when I sometimes have the wit to be alert to my students, that it is the best, not the poorest, students who are likely to reach out for needed help through such disguised gambits.

Conclusion

Shepherding of families through direct contact is always important. This is not needed only by those in overt trouble; it is often needed precisely by those with the greatest defenses against admitting their need. So far as direct shepherding is concerned, the problem is seldom simply one of the marriage and family and most often requires dealing with the inner conflicts and anxieties of individual persons. There are occasions and ways, however, in which counseling with a couple can be reasonably certain to do no harm and to have a fair chance of accomplishing some good. Since shepherding is not confined to one-to-one relationships, what is done in sermons, in public discussions, and even in committee meeting may often mean more to family welfare than the pastor has usually thought. However briefly, all these have been illustrated.

Space does not permit a discussion of the shepherding of people prior to marriage—a subject of great importance on which very little really effective literature is available.

About this we can say only so much. Two functions are inevitably involved in discussion by a pastor with couples who wish to be married. One is the representative function: is he justified—all things considered, especially his representation of the Christian community—in performing this ceremony? Second, can he give the pastoral help now needed for the better understanding of the meaning of marriage and the family from the Christian point of view, and so impress the couple with the relevance and realism of the Christian family that the church will be the first place they come for help later on when it is needed? There is no *necessary* contradiction between these functions, but neither is there a guarantee of automatic harmony. The spelling out of these functions of Christian shepherding is greatly needed.

V. SHEPHERDING AND THE CLASS STRUCTURE

If we want to help and shepherd someone, the first thing we must do is to move inside his frame of reference so that we understand, to the degree he permits, why he sees and feels as he does. We are sympathetic (or empathetic, as some use the term) to his point of view in the sense that we do, internally, try to grasp and to accept that he feels as he does, granted the conditions that have brought him to it. We are not necessarily sympathetic to his point of view in the sense of agreeing on its normative character.

Our thesis in this chapter is that one important factor needing to be taken into account in order to get inside the frame of reference of the person rests in what he assumes, believes, and has experienced in relation to the class structure of our society. Such general knowledge, like any other general knowledge, is never a substitute for specific understanding in specific instances. But in the same sense in which knowledge of internal psychodynamics can prepare us for understanding people according to their own frame of reference, so can a dynamic knowledge of the class structure and its effect upon persons.

It is only in relatively recent years that serious studies have been made of the class structure in our allegedly classless society. There are some understandable reasons for this delay. Whatever its divisions and inequities, the structure of our society is not necessarily fixed in relation to specific individuals. In the absence of a fixed caste form of class, and with that positive aspect of American society in which everyone is trying to rise and be raised, the actual operations of class for a long time evaded systematic scrutiny. But in recent years we have had several systematic general studies.[1] Other studies on particular subjects—for instance, on sexual behavior and on drinking mores—have made use of the general findings and have in return enriched them.

To a good many people the whole idea of talking of the class structure is repugnant—suggestive of some kind of un-Americanism if not actually of Marxism. Of course such notions are mistaken. What we mean, above all else, by the class structure is that some people in our society come to take certain things for granted which are, in many instances, quite different from what other people take for granted. These differences in assumptions affect the inner experiencing of the two groups as well as the outward institutionalizing of the two kinds of patterns.

Income level and economic status are certainly involved in the class structure, but they are not the sole factors, and often not the most important ones. Educational level is often more important, and so is the type of work in which one engages. As we all know, race and national origin unfortunately are often dominant factors in determining class status.

Trying to get an overview of this matter of class structure, there seem to be three areas that carry the largest implications for Christian shepherding. We shall deal with these in turn.

Acceptance or Rejection

The first thing done by the class structure is to affect vitally and basically a person's relative sense of acceptance or rejection. To put it another way, this is a basic factor conditioning his sense of personal identity or of personal existence. Let us move at once to cases.

Lloyd Warner tells the poignant story of Priscilla Sellers of Jonesville.[2] Priscilla's father, a respectable workingman, was awakened one day by an unaccustomed noise that sounded like crying. It was afternoon, and Mr. Sellers hoped to sleep a bit longer before going to work on the night shift. He knew Priscilla's mother was doing the laundry and ironing at the home of Mr. Vollmers, his boss, and that his two older children were at work. Priscilla was of course at high school.

Pursuing the noise, Mr. Sellers found Priscilla sobbing quietly under the bed in her own room. She liked and respected her father, and did her best to explain to him how she felt. The whole trouble, she said, was that she was no longer accepted in high school. "Everyone up there hates me," she continued, and she gave chapter and verse.

All through grammar school, her father reminded her, she had been an excellent student and had also been happy. Yes, returned Priscilla, then she played with all the girls including those from the hill, even Sylvia Vollmers, the daughter of father's boss. But in the eighth grade all that began to change, and it grew progressively worse in high school. Just that morning Priscilla had spoken to Sylvia Vollmers in school, but Sylvia, without acknowledging what Priscilla had said, turned to two other girls and made a comment Priscilla could not hear, whereupon all three girls looked at Priscilla and laughed.

There was a club called the PFP's, Priscilla went on, and all the girls from the hill belonged. But the worst thing, said Priscilla, was the drum majorette business. The school principal had called her in and said that, because she had recently skipped school, she would have to give up being a drum majorette. It was true, Priscilla admitted, that she had played hookey several times. It just became so hard she and some of the other girls couldn't take it, and they had stayed away. But about the drum majorette business—the hill girls had had secret practice sessions, refusing to tell Priscilla when and where they were to be held, and then at official rehearsals she looked awkward because she did not know the new figures.

Priscilla concluded, with a poignancy that is not well conveyed by this abbreviated account, that she was going to quit school. Her father urged her to reconsider. He pointed out that her older brother and sister had both been smart also but had quit school, and she was the last one in the family who had a chance. In Warner's story, Mr. Sellers is then shown talking to a successful man friend who had risen from the ranks. This friend is sympathetic, but prides himself on being realistic. When he hears that Priscilla has quit school, he says, "Yes, that's exactly the way it goes here in Jonesville."

Lest anyone have the illusion that going to church could have cured all this, Priscilla stopped going to church before she quit going to school, because the other kids made her feel that she did not belong there.

At this point the Warner story stops, and we can only speculate about Priscilla's future. She must of course go to work. With her small amount of education, and with no particular skills, she will be unlikely to get much of a job. And, feeling as rejected as she does, it is improbable that she will develop those abilities in human relations now so much sought after by personnel departments. Priscilla will be at least secretly resentful of those above her, and perhaps overly grateful for acceptance by those on her own level. She may indeed possess personal qualities that will allow her, on her own or through marriage, to rise in the class scale, but the chances are against it. All through her life Priscilla is likely to feel cheated; or, in order to avoid that feeling, to turn it into resentment. She may, as many Priscillas have done, even become a champion of just those customs and conventions that war upon the customs of the upper crust.

Every church contains Priscillas. In justice to this church, we may note that she was always officially welcome there. It was not officially an upper class church. But we may well ask: Who was looking the other way when Priscilla and some of her other working class friends were being frozen out of the church school? If we try to blame it on the church-school teacher, she can shift the blame to the superintendent and note that nothing was ever said to her about this kind of thing. The superintendent can refer to the pastor and say the same. Since I have yet to see a discourse on the class structure in any leadership training material, I doubt that anything is gained by blaming the pastor, for he can retort that his theological education never prepared him for things like this. But plainly, blame or no blame, once the family and the school had failed to handle this situation, the one other resource was the church. With Priscilla it failed. We may thank the sheer grace of God, through humane and warm people, that it does not always fail teen-agers. Any pastor, with even a small grasp of what it means to have Priscilla's type of experience, can certainly do something positive with his church-school staff.

We might look at some of the possible occasions when a

Priscilla might appeal for help to her pastor. On occasion, if he has proved unusually understanding, she might even consult him about leaving school. But the chances are, if she ever consults him, it will not be in direct reference to the class structure. Some day she and her fiancé may ask him to marry them. Will he make this only a formal occasion, or will he strengthen both Priscilla and the forthcoming marriage by some insightful counseling not unaware of the class pressures in the background? Still later, he may find Priscilla is a member of the church while her husband is not. Will he simply order a sales talk for the husband, or will he be sensitive to the possibility that Priscilla may not have given up while her husband has done so? The possibilities are endless, and hardly require enumeration. The point is that any pastoral care at any time, whatever its immediate occasion, must be sensitive to the power politics of the class structure in the background, or it will miss very important dimensions of understanding and helping the people.

We have concentrated here on Priscilla as one rejected by those who had once accepted her. We might have asked about Sylvia Vollmers, the boss's daughter, who demonstrated being among the in-group by placing Priscilla on the out. Every church has its Sylvias, at all stages of their development. At first glance we are inclined to be simply indignant about Sylvia and think that the pastoral care she needs is a good talking-to. Even if we transcend the prudential consideration that Sylvia's father is probably a member of the board, and even if we are wise enough to talk with Sylvia without wholly rejecting her, we are likely to be baffled. She will tell us that Priscilla was in with a bad crowd, that she was playing hookey from school, that she had fallen down in her schoolwork, and probably that the boys in Priscilla's group were, well, not nice boys at all. In other words, the Sylvias of this world have at their disposal all the rationalizations needed to live comfortably with pride.

Can one ever get to them? At times one can, although rarely by denunciation. Sometimes the pattern is so deep and, we might add, so externally successful, that nothing will avail. But when two conditions are present, there is always some chance. The first is the clear recognition that he who has need for many rationalizations has some potential feeling of guilt, or bad conscience, that may under conditions of acceptance be appealed to. The other is sufficient knowledge of the psychological and sociological dynamics that one cannot be thrown off the scent by even the most clever rationalizations. Homiletically speaking, I suggest that the parable of the talents may be interpreted, among other ways, so as to say something constructive both to Priscilla and to Sylvia.

Right or Wrong

The first thing done by the class structure, we have noted, is to affect basically and vitally the person's sense of acceptance or rejection, his sense of his personal identity, and even of his existence.

The second thing done by the class structure is moral teaching. More specifically, class patterns permeate people, as it were by osmosis, so that they learn to take for granted that which their class takes for granted. Some things are assumed to be right, or at least natural and necessary, while other things are assumed to be wrong, or unnatural and dispensable.

It is just at this point that an especially important contribution to our understanding has been made by the much misunderstood studies of sex behavior conducted by the late Alfred C. Kinsey and his colleagues.[3] Findings about the significance of social class as affecting attitudes toward sex behavior are all the more important, since they occupied only a minor place in Kinsey's original hypotheses. Among Amercian men, Kinsey's findings show beyond question that the most significant differences in attitudes toward sex and sex behavior are functions of the class structure. Such class-based differences are many times more influential than, for instance, church membership, or its absence.

Kinsey found that men who came from lower-class homes, especially as represented by there having been little formal education in this stratum, tended to regard premarital sexual intercourse as natural, inevitable, and more or less like a flood. Almost regardless of other possible teaching, they tended not to regard this matter as a moral issue. They did not decide it, but felt it was decided for them. In striking contrast, men from upper-level homes, as measured by formal education of the stratum, felt that premarital sexual relations were always a moral issue, regardless of whether decision was made pro or con. The upper-level group accepted nudity in the home—for example, if a child should see his father or mother in the bathtub. In contrast, lower-level homes felt nudity was unnatural, often including in this stricture even sexual intercourse between husband and wife.

In the group that had had education and class status midway between the persons who stopped in grade school and those who went into college, Kinsey found an odd conflict between the upper-level and lower-level patterns. This group was most vocal and clear about the evils of sex—

for example, about premarital sexual relationships or about homosexuality. It was most insistent about rigidity of right and wrong in behavior. Yet, on many counts, the actual behavior of this group tended most to contradict what it said —for example, about homosexuality. The attitude of this group is what I have called a respectability-restraint attitude. It is trying hard to keep out of the lower-level patterns. But it finds this difficult because it still secretly believes, along with the lower-level groups, that sex is a flood. Hence its dikes must be built high and rigid.

In regard to women the Kinsey findings require more subtle interpretation than in relation to men. For in terms of actual behavior that can be counted in terms of incidents, Kinsey did not find the striking differences among women of different social classes that he did of men. My interpretation, based on careful study of his findings, plus other data, is that the same patterns are at work but that they result in smaller differences in terms of overt behavior. Their significance is attitudinal.

To sum up, no other single factor so affects what people assume to be right or wrong, natural or unnatural, in sex attitudes and behavior as the class in which they have been reared. For good or for ill, this is a fact.

Special study has been made also on drinking patterns among social classes, of which a very quick summary is possible.[4] In upper-upper-class circles, the use of alcohol is not a moral issue. At least a little use of alcohol is regarded as a normal part of civilized living, but drunkenness is frowned on to the point of ostracism.

The lower upper class, or *nouveaux riches,* also accept alcohol as a part of gracious living. But, lacking the built-in social controls of the traditional aristocracy, actual drinking is often a very different matter.

The upper middle class, in imitation of the aristocracy, ordinarily drinks a little. It also wishes to show it has transcended the no-drinking moralism of the lower middle class. Since the main psychological characteristic of the upper middle class is ambition, it may drink little or nothing, in service of that ambition for prudential reasons; or it may, harassed with anxiety, drink far too much.

The lower middle class is against drinking in principle, although by no means always so in practice. There is some evidence to suggest that the greatest proportion of alcoholics comes from this group that most strongly stands against any drinking. This evidence is, however, not conclusive. Some of the antidrinking stand of this group has come from its sense of having moved out of the lower classes. So far as it is moving toward the upper middle class, the antidrinking stand tends to change.

In both segments of the lower class drinking tends to be confined to groups of men or of women but not both together. Here is where the saloon differs from the cocktail lounge in general pattern, even if, behaviorally, there is often little to choose between them.

Let us return to our main concern, how Christian shepherding is conditioned by the class structure. Here we have dealt with illustrative attitudes toward selected issues of right and wrong.

The most obvious conclusion is that one is doomed to fail in his shepherding if he underestimates the extent to which his own class patterns make it difficult to see things from the inside point of view of someone whose class patterns are different. It may be all the more difficult if his own class has imperialized its patterns and, as has sometimes been done, has assured him they are the sole and exclusive Christian patterns. The general process, of which putting Mother Hubbards on natives is a specific instance, is not confined to the South Seas. But even in the absence of this imperialism, it is difficult to move sympathetically within the perspective of someone who assumes quite different patterns from those in which we believe. My conviction, in relation to something like sex attitudes, for example, is that no actually existing class attitude is in accord with the implications of the Christian position and that no attitude is so wholly wrong that there is no place for it to make contact with the Christian position. All this means that dealing with the class structure is not simply a matter of understanding the pressures on other fellows. It is also, and even more crucially, understanding those assumptions that have come from our class pattern that we ourselves make and which, unless we do understand their origin, will serve as obstacles to our ministry to the many sorts and conditions and classes of men.

Fulfillment or Service

The third area I shall mention in which class status affects personal attitudes is the relation between fulfillment and service. This can also be stated in terms of the assumptions about the character and meaning of human relationships.

It is a good deal more difficult to demonstrate, much less to prove, a connection between class structure and attitudes on the relation of fulfillment to service, than it has been with the two areas previously discussed. More of this material is hypothetical. If true at all, however, it is very important for our concern. Hence it seems worth some hypothesizing and speculating. We may at least make the discussion concrete through a case.

A minister was consulted by a woman of middle age who was a member of his church. A married woman whose children had reached adulthood, she held a supervisory position of a white-collar type in a relatively large business. She was tall, immaculately groomed, and what is often called "handsome." There were no indications that she had any of the traits that the culture defines as masculine and which it finds objectionable in career women. So far as the minister knew, Mrs. Supervisor had maintained a good home for her husband and children, and engaged in her job because of her interest in it, not primarily to keep the family budget afloat.

She had sought out the pastor, Mrs. Supervisor said, because she was concerned about certain relationships in her work. She gave much detail about relationships with her boss, about some prounion and antiunion tactics that were going on, and about her own work of supervising relatively unskilled girls. Her coming to the pastor, she said, was because she wondered if she herself might be at fault to some extent in the immediate situation, as she had just been passed over for promotion and the higher job given to a man with far less experience than she.

In the course of discussing many things, she finally told of a misunderstanding she had recently had with one of the girls working under her direction. Some of the other girls had come to her, she said, and complained about this girl, alleging that she came to work with a heavy and unpleasant body odor that the other girls found offensive. Mrs. Supervisor had called the girl into her office, found her resistive to discussing the matter at all; but after persistent discussion, had concluded that underpants were the offending member, and had offered specific advice on how they could be washed out each night. She had tried hard, she continued, to understand the girl, but had been met only with negative response even to the point of ill-concealed anger. Later, she said, she had found that this girl lived in a cold-water flat and that she had been divorced. Of course Mrs. Supervisor knew that the wages paid her were barely enough to subsist on.

But this time the probable nature of the difficulty was reasonably clear to the pastor. He saw also that Mrs. Supervisor had all the data she needed for the answer; and he surmised that her coming to him, as a pastor, suggested that something in her was more ready to arrive at the unflattering answer than she, in her head, realized. As he proceded, although with caution, this turned out to be true.

Finally Mrs. Supervisor said, "I can see now what I should have seen all along. I have simply been looking at everything through middle-class eyes. Dirt and smell are offensive. And even though I tried to understand Alice, it literally never occurred to me that these could mean to her something utterly different from what they meant to me. Looking at things now from her point of view, I can see why she was indignant at me. She is discouraged and depressed. Her marriage has failed and she is alone. She has a job, but it is just enough to get by on. She hates the cold-water flat she has to live in. Most of the time she thinks what's the use? And there I was being fastidious about underpants."

Mrs. Supervisor may of course have other problems than that which emerged in this discussion. But basically she is a woman of kindheartedness. Yet she had no notion that her looking into other people was filtered through a very narrow pair of spectacles.

Let us look at her assumptions about fulfillment, and about service, and their relationship. She felt she was competent, was therefore giving proper service. For this she felt she ought to be rewarded, which would have meant her fulfilment. But the incident of the girl brought to even her own attention a class-based rigidity which no doubt affected all her relationships. In a higher position she would be untrustworthy; for, finally, her rightness, her giving proper service, would be judged in terms of moralistic rigidity, at the expense of business efficiency on the one side, and of warm human understanding on the other. Her conception of fulfillment was as reward for specific service rendered. But because of the rigidity, the fulfillment contained no more spontaneity than did the service. This was not quite the whole story, or else she would not have consulted the pastor. In that sense something in her as a person was beginning to transcend the class pressures. But her conception of both fulfillment and service was legalistic, and there was a purely formal relationship between them. Note that this attitude not only prevented her from any spontaneous fulfillment, it also inhibited some naturally warm impulses to help the girl with the dirty underpants. The failure to permit any spontaneity about fulfillment blinded her to it in terms of service, and *vice versa*.

Long before our modern formal studies of class structure, social observers have pointed out, on the one hand, how often the self-made man lacks sympathy for those less successful than himself, and, on the other, how great leaders of the common people very often come from the aristocracy. Our knowledge of the class structure suggests why this may be true, however often it is not true in individual cases. To the self-made man service may seem a concession based on weakness. It may, prudentially, be necessary. But fulfillment has rested on being the captain of one's soul, working hard, and taking risks. Anything else is weakness. It is the part of oneself to which no concessions have been made. Why, then, make these concessions to others?

The aristocrat may, on the other hand, be unlike the Marxist picture of him, serving only his own privilege. Secure as a Winston Churchill in his own status, he may have the ability to penetrate with understanding into that of others. Fulfillment and service may have an interpenetrating relationship, from his point of view. He need not confuse them, or assume an automatic harmony between them. But he may find much fulfillment in service so that service to him is strength not weakness. He may even be wise enough to recognize that, if he had been granted no fulfillment, he could not serve.

What of our girl in the cold-water flat? How does she look on fulfillment and service? To her service is drudgery, and such small fulfillment as she has is purely marginal. The last thing she could conceive would be that service and fulfillment might actually go together. How, indeed, could she feel otherwise?

Our discussion of the effect of class patterns upon conceptions of service and fulfillment has been couched perhaps too much in terms of occupation, but we believe it possible to generalize from this type of consideration. And all this seems very important for pastoral care.

Normatively, Christian faith and Christian ethics hold that fulfillment should be a by-product of service; but that the service proceeds from a fulfillment not of our own making—that it is the work of God's grace, and that therefore the ability to serve is, finally, testimony to the grace of God.

Would not this tend to look quite different to Mrs. Supervisor, to the girl in the cold-water flat, to the self-made man, and to Winston Churchill? If called upon to help any of them, would not our pastoral task be difficult to the point of impossibility unless we recognized differences of this order? If we simply railed against selfishness, or rigidity, or legalism, or moralism, we would fail to establish relationship. If we could only discuss relaxing, surrendering, letting go, or relying on grace, it is doubtful if the connections would be better established. Still more remote, however true, might be erudite discussions of the relationship between love and justice. The place might come, and hopefully it would, when such matters would become relevant. But if there is no toe hold, they remain foreign. That hold is often to be found in insights into the way class patterns condition one's assumptions about the relationship of fulfillment and service.

Class Mobility

However briefly, we must note two other facts about the class structure in relation to Christian shepherding. The first of these is social mobility. Not only is there a large amount of individual social mobility in our society; the whole current trend is toward upward mobility by the population as a whole. Nowhere is this seen more vividly than in the increased number and proportion of people who have higher education. People who go to college accept college values and college assumptions about many crucial things. More and more workingmen belong, classwise, to the middle class. More and more persons in the lower middle class are moving to the lower reaches of the upper middle class. The whole trend is upward in an hierarchical sense.

We tend to evaluate this general trend as good when it means, for example, that more people have more education. But we tend to appraise it as bad when, for instance, more people are tempted to accept the drinking patterns of the class into which they are moving rather than the patterns of that which they are leaving. We cannot understand our individual people unless we take individual as well as general social mobility into account. It may be much harder for a person to deal critically with the assumptions of the class into which he is moving than it is to deal with those of the class from which he is emerging. In a time of general upward mobility, we have to be sensitive to the thrust as well as to the background.

We may note also that—especially in a time of widespread upward mobility—individual downward mobility assumes a special character. To his class such a person may be an object of scorn or of pity, and there is often not much difference between these. The professor's son who becomes a mechanic, or the physician's daughter who marries a factory foreman, has special problems. They are altogether too likely to take into themselves the judgment of their new class, in spite of outward defiance, and to be embittered, or weak, or self-defeating as a result.

Man, Woman, and Class

The final thing on which we shall comment is the effect of the class structure on conceptions of masculinity and femininity. There are, to be sure, general conceptions in our culture that transcend the class structure. The unathletic boy has a hard time—often too hard a time—in any stratum of our society. So has the very intelligent girl. But there are class differences nonetheless.

Space permits my dealing with only one class. By the middle class, especially the lower middle class, masculinity and femininity tend to be rigidly defined. A boy with artistic leanings has a difficult time in this setting. So does a girl who believes she may not want to marry. In terms of intellectual interests, men must confine themselves to external things. Only women are permitted to take seriously the internal look. Higher in the class scale there is more allowance for individuality, and in the lower groups the distinctions are more functional. All we can do here is to suggest that such distinctions exist, and that pastoral care not alert to them will be irrelevant.

By cultural standards, Christian thought and Christian life are neither masculine nor feminine. If Christian thought were occupied wholly externally, denying the need for an inward look, or for tenderness, or for humility (which the culture regards as feminine), violence would be done to the faith. And if Christian thought should look only to a spirit within, and should set aside all objective and external considerations (which the culture regards as masculine), the faith would also be distorted. There are times when even theologians are more affected by class assumptions of this kind than they know.

Conclusion

This has been an all-too-brief consideration of the class structure in relation to Christian shepherding. The main point has been simple—that knowledge of the pressures that class puts on persons and the assumptions it gives them is an important preliminary to being able to establish contact with many sorts and conditions of men. We have discussed this in three main points and two subsidiary ones. The main ones were, what class does to patterns of acceptance or rejection, what it does to conceptions of right and wrong, and what it does to ideas about the relationship between fulfillment and service. The subsidiary points, on which we touched but lightly, were the fact of class mobility, and the class assumptions about masculinity and femininity.

Knowledge of the kind we have been setting forth is, it may be well to note, mostly regarded as masculine by the culture. The actual process by which we attempt to get understandingly within the frame of reference of another person is, by cultural definition, feminine. Valuable as this kind of knowledge may be in helping us to clear blind spots from our own eyes and to see those of others, it is not in itself a substitute for the tender and solicitous concern that is always the essence of Christian shepherding. If one were interested in what a person's class had done to him, but had no interest in the person from the person's own point of view, he would be misusing valuable knowledge in the interests of what could be traced, finally, to unassimilated class pressures of his own.

VI. SHEPHERDING ORGANIZATION MEN

The "organization man" has been made known with popular effectiveness by William F. Whyte, Jr.[1] Coming just before him was David Riesman's "outer-directed" man.[2] In the forties Erich Fromm taught us about the man with the "marketing orientation" to life.[3] The essence of these conceptions is the same. They all suggest that contemporary man is becoming a peculiarly subtle kind of conformist. Each of them emphasizes certain features of this conformity. What impresses Whyte is the erosion of uniqueness. Riesman believes that inner convictions are being lost. Fromm sees modern man as unable to take initiative and direct himself.

Even a generation ago something similar was being stated by Carl Jung and Otto Rank. Modern western man, Jung held, has lost touch with his own depths, because he has given up the collective resources that previously served both as avenues to these depths and as protections against his being swallowed by them.[4] These avenues were mainly religion and the church, but also had to do with art, mythology, and other things. Exceptional individuals may find their depths as individuals again, through such difficult processes as psychological therapy. But most men, Jung held, confuse their selfhood with their "persona"—that layer of personality that is in contact with the outer world and which reflects its expectations.

With less subtlety but more prophetic vigor Otto Rank saw most modern men degenerating into a normal-average type that made equally impossible true neurosis or creative expression.[5] Man who is not attempting to exercise his potential creativity, according to Rank, is man truncated. To be sure, there are risks in doing so. Neurosis in its true sense, he felt, is creativity improperly expressed. But even the neurotic has not lost his creativity, as has the normal-average man.

By all these avenues we return to organization man. He has lost his uniqueness and does not know it. He no longer has real inner convictions but thinks he has. He cannot take initiative but believes he does. He does not even know he has depths, much less what they are. He has buried in a napkin the priceless talent of creativity, with the doubtful gain of avoiding neurosis.

Are these charges true? Are most modern men subtly becoming conformist while unaware of it? That is a question I am not prepared to argue on a statistical basis. An appalling number of things that would support the organization-man thesis immediately strike the eye. But there are surely other trends as well. The story is going the rounds of the reporter who wanted to smear the organization-man label on a corporation; and who, after some months in its toils, gave up his effort because the respect for individuality seemed unfortunately to be true.

I am personally much inclined to believe that the organization man thesis represents the dominant characterological trend of our time. Be that as it may, there is such a trend affecting many, if not necessarily most, people. It is of these, and the ministry of shepherding to them, that we will speak.

With some sections of our population, the first impulse on hearing about organization man is to denounce the whole hypothesis. The reaction of persons like ourselves is dif-

98

ferent. To the extent that there is truth in it as a factual description, we say to ourselves, we must denounce what produces it. Men are not automatons. They are not to lose moral or any other kind of responsibility. If the conformism is subtle, all the more reason for condemning it. We may go on to add that this kind of conformism, religiously speaking, is idolatry.

All this may, in a way, be true, but it is not the whole truth. There is a very real danger that too quick denunciation of organization men will blind us to that organization man who constitutes some part of ourselves. The secret appeal of the organization-man thesis is that one who appreciates the truth of the thesis is relatively certain that he himself is not an organization man. Very well, he is not —as a whole man. But if the trends go as deep into the fabric of interpersonal life as all these observers suggest, then it would be strange indeed if anyone remained wholly unscathed.

Ecclesiastical Organization Men

If we take the organization-man concept seriously, then we must concede at once that the character (or ideals) of the particular organization is no automatic guarantee against organization men. Just as power may corrupt as quickly in the church as elsewhere, so organization men may arise as speedily in ecclesiastical as in other forms. From the point of view of the real meaning of the church, organization men are undesirable because they are idolatrous, giving to an institution that loyalty which should be reserved for God alone. Yet no church is without them, and being a churchman does not guarantee any of us that we will not develop organization-man tendencies.

There are some rather obvious ways in which the church on Main Street, of every denomination, tends, against its own ideals, to foster organization men. For example, programs originally designed to meet important needs may become, for all practical purposes, ends in themselves, until the "successful" minister or church is that which can produce the most statistics in the proper areas. He who has nearly lost the ability to criticize the means in the light of the ends is close to becoming an organization man.

Another obvious matrix for the ecclesiastical organization man may grow in perverted fashion out of the sound maxim that the Christian message should be presented so as to meet human needs. The maxim *is* correct. He who is entirely unaware when his communication of the message has failed is not performing his Christian function. But, in moving away from irrelevance, pastor or church may sometimes move toward mere popularity—judging the effectiveness of the communication solely in terms of its appeal and neglecting the issues of truth. When this is done, the gospel is diluted. No one is offended, but neither is anyone saved.

A discerning reader of this manuscript has suggested a third way in which ecclesiastical organization men may be produced. This had not originally occurred to me, but I believe it merits consideration. This reader asked, "Is it possible that some of us have chosen the ministry as our vocation and profession partly because we do a lot of living in glass houses—and thereby are relieved of responsibility for some aspects of our own behavior?" I am sure there are individual ministers to whom this applies. And perhaps many more of us would have to acknowledge at least the measure of truth in it as applying to ourselves.

In addition to these ways by which organization men are

produced in the church, many others could be mentioned. Some church officials appear to be selected primarily because they have never rocked any boat. And most churches seem to have a kind of stereotyped picture of a minister, which may in fact severely cripple the best development of many ministers. The fact is that different ministers may have different basic "styles," things that most awaken them and stimulate them to better work over the whole of the ministry. It would be tragic if but one basic style were permitted. The man truly awakened through preaching should not look down on the man whose ministry has come alive through pastoral care, so long as the preacher improves his pastoral care and the shepherd improves his preaching. In so far as our picture of the ministry is a stereotype, it tends to produce ecclesiastical organization men.

The main point we have made is that being Christians or Protestants or ministers does not automatically prevent us from being organization men. Even though we may renounce this in its crude forms, that gives no guarantee that the seven organizational devils will not enter us and make us more organizational than before.

We may summarize. If a minister is an organization man, it is because he permits the actual church to have heteronomous control over him. He forfeits both autonomy and the fulfillment of autonomy through theonomy, to use Paul Tillich's phrases.[6] To the extent that the church is true to its own self-critical principle, he may be saved from some of the worst forms of the organization man, but his very existence in his heteronomous state threatens the capacity of the church to remain self-critical.

How can we shepherd the ecclesiastical organization man? Let it first be clear that attack and denunciation are unlikely to do any good. He will make his defenses stronger, or he will shift the content of his heteronomous loyalty without altering its tone. In either event he will be more fixed than before in the organization man pattern.

On the other hand, we will not help him if we reward him for his acts and thoughts of conformity. This would confuse heteronomy with theonomy.

We must first make contact. That will prove very difficult unless we recognize that there is something of the organization man in us also. With that realization, we can begin to see things from his point of view. It would be strange indeed if under these circumstances we did not find that organization men, even in the ministry, emerge from weakness and fear. Will this recognition always de-organize such men? By no means. The patterns may be too old and have gone too deep. But if one wants to help the organization men who are still helpable, he is far more likely to accomplish it in this way than by the ways we have rejected—of denunciation on the one side, or reward on the other.

As a matter of fact, there is often a kind of secret alliance between denunciation and reward. We can denounce conformist trends to everything except what we regard as the proper cause, and then reward people for showing just those trends toward the one right cause. This is precisely like the secret alliance that Freud noted between the super-ego and the id, between the conscience and the impulses.

Since organization men, even in the ministry, are products of fear and insecurity, shepherding needs to involve helping them to find the needed security. Their need for security, and for the avoidance of risk, genuine initiative, and the exercise of creativity, is shown in their being organization men. What they need is a base of security from which

102

risk, initiative, and creativity can and must be exercised. This is not, be it noted, a matter of denouncing all needs for security. Only the secure man can feel anxious when he should. So only the man with the right security base can afford to transcend conformity.

Lay Organization Men

If what we have said about ourselves as clergy is true, then we have some principles by which to approach the shepherding of laymen who are organization men. Although there may indeed be many organization men who never go to church, the fact is that the main current pattern of the organization man includes his having at least a tenuous connection with the Gothic building on Main Street.

Let us look first at the young married group of the type described by Whyte, who live in places like Park Forest. During the day no men are visible. They leave early in the morning, get back relatively late in the evening, and are at home only on week ends. The women are occupied in child care and talk with immediate neighbors. Every court is a playground. Hardly anyone expects to live there permanently. There is little sense of the larger community. Most residents know few people outside their own court area unless they have met them in church.

Where conformity is less in mass production than at Park Forest, Sunday, and often weekday, nurseries have been avenues by which young married people have come into the church. The architecture of Park Forest makes this less necessary. Yet the Park Forest churches are full of both adults and children. Speaking of the country generally, there has never been a time when there were so many young married people in the church.

We have sometimes underestimated the extent to which young married people are busy. From front door to work and return, the young married man puts in almost as long a weekday as did the farmer of a generation ago. His wife, to be sure, is benefited by laborsaving devices; and in Park Forest types of situation, she exchanges baby-sitting service with other wives. But her relative freedom from physical labor in the form of washboards, shucking peas, or weaving cloth tends to go into watching her children so they will at all times have good social adjustment. As a reducer of anxiety, watching children play is not in it with a washboard.

Where shepherding is sought by young married people, every effective instance of it will point beyond itself. That is, it will transcend the problem that occasioned the contact. The recognition of a problem, whatever its nature, and the readiness to mention it to the minister is in itself moving beyond the perspective of organization men. It is a mark of initiative and creativity.

There is much evidence that the period involving entrance into early middle age is more decisive and more critical than we have usually recognized. It is in this period that we find peak figures for alcoholism, for adultery among educated people, for illness with a large psychic component, and for many other types of personal and social ills. As Carl Jung noted a generation ago, the movement from the first to the second half of life is not heralded by many external changes; its crisis is internal, and for that reason is often ignored.

Developmentally speaking, there is no crisis in early middle life that has not been latent during the young adult years. But in the mode of modern young adult living, the busyness, the child preoccupation, and the scramble to get ahead all tend to hold in abeyance any latent sense of meaninglessness, or uncreativity, or of fear that produces conformity. Activity and ambition make the period tolerable, even though deep chasms may lie beneath the surface. This is all the more reason why the shepherd may be alert, regardless of the specific problem, to the young adult or to the couple who are ready to talk with him. He cannot be concerned solely with proper solution of the presented problem when he has an opportunity to foster the very qualities that will make transition to middle age, later on, tolerable and productive. William H. Whyte notes that the demand for counseling by ministers tends to be high in suburbs with a heavy population of young married people.[7] The question is: What use will be made of these opportunities?

The meaning of this needs some demonstration, and it is well to begin by showing how a well-intentioned pastor can unwittingly help produce organization men and women. Young Mrs. Zendt and her husband have a son who is one year old. Twice before the present pastoral interview she has talked with young Pastor Zarvis about baptism, has requested literature about it and about what the particular denomination stands for in general. Pastor Zarvis knew that Mrs. Zendt had once been a Roman Catholic but that her husband had been reared as a Protestant. On this occasion Mrs. Zendt called on Pastor Zarvis, returned the books, and the following conversation took place:

MRS. ZENDT: I meant to call and see you before now.
PASTOR ZARVIS: It's good to see you this time.

MRS. ZENDT: I think that we have decided to have our little boy baptized in your church.

PASTOR ZARVIS: You have looked over the books I gave you?

MRS. ZENDT: Yes, I read all of the small one and parts of the larger one. I think they told me all that I need to know.

PASTOR ZARVIS: I hope that you noticed the simple confession of faith that we use in our church. I think that is what you said you desired in a religion?

MRS. ZENDT: That is true. It contains all the things that matter, but it gives a person the right and duty to think many things through for himself.

PASTOR ZARVIS: We think that in doing this we make religion more a part of a person's life because then it is really his.

MRS. ZENDT: I believe your church has the answer to the problems in our family. We have talked about religion a lot recently, and the decision to have our child baptized in your church means much to us.

PASTOR ZARVIS: Such a decision in religion should mean much to every person.

MRS. ZENDT: Yes, but frequently it does not. Most people don't worry too much about religion. My religion is very important to me. I have had to do a lot of thinking about it. You know that I was Catholic, but I don't think I told you that my family was very strict in its religion. One of my relatives is a priest.

PATOR ZARVIS: Then your decision to break with the Catholic Church is a big one for you to take.

MRS. ZENDT: Yes, my Catholic faith was a strong one for many years. I went to Catholic schools. I never got along too well there, though. I seemed to get into trouble. But they did suggest that I be a nun. I came very close, but I think that all the time there must have been some great problem about my convictions.

PASTOR ZARVIS: You will have some conflict with your family when you do join our church?

MRS. ZENDT: Of course I will. But I guess that it all started when

I married. We ran away and were married by a justice of the peace. But my family has sort of got over all that. Now when I do really change my religion, I don't know what they will think.

PASTOR ZARVIS: It always does present something of a problem.

MRS. ZENDT: Have you had many Catholics join your church since you have been here?

PASTOR ZARVIS: Yes, a good number. Probably a majority of the people who have come into our church here have either made a definite break at the time of their joining, or have come from homes of Catholic background.

MRS. ZENDT: Then I guess that other people do make the adjustments.

PASTOR ZARVIS: Yes, at first it may make a serious break with the families, but it seems that time has a way of making for peace. The important things in personality stand out stronger than religious conflicts.

MRS. ZENDT: I am not sure that I will feel at home in your church. Your service is different.

PASTOR ZARVIS: Our service is very simple. But we strive to make it worshipful. In this also I think you will find more room for each person to apply it to himself.

MRS. ZENDT: I do like simplicity. What date could we set for our service? When do other people do it?

PASTOR ZARVIS: It can come either after the Sunday morning service, or you can have a service of your own.

MRS. ZENDT: I think a private service would be better.

PASTOR ZARVIS: Then you can get in touch with me, and we will have it when it is convenient for you.

By no means everything done by Pastor Zarvis in this relationship is to be reprimanded. There were times—for instance when he said, "Then a decision to break with the Catholic Church is a big one for you to take."—when he does genuinely try to get inside Mrs. Zendt's frame of reference, and thus to aid her in exercising the thoughtful and creative initiative that has brought her to him in the first place.

But the pastor's overall dealing is otherwise. As Mrs. Zendt makes clear, the tentative decision she and her husband have made to have their son baptized in a Protestant church, and the consequent and antecedent decision to affiliate themselves with that church, have not emerged easily. Especially has Mrs. Zendt had to do some hard thinking. When the chips were down, Pastor Zarvis took none of this very seriously. When Mrs. Zendt, in understandable perturbation, indicates that she is troubled about what her family will think when she becomes a Protestant, Pastor Zarvis evades the issue altogether and says, "It always does present something of a problem." That is organization man thinking with a vengeance, right down to the statistics. When Mrs. Zendt, trying to assure herself, says she guesses other people do live through it, Pastor Zarvis avers that "time has a way of making for peace." This virtually denies her the right to be concerned. But if she had not been concerned, she would not have taken the initiative and done the thinking that make her joining the church just the opposite of the organization man's.

The worst bit of all arrives when Mrs. Zendt says, "I am not sure that I will feel at home in your church. Your service is different." The pastor replies, "Our service is very simple. But we strive to make it worshipful. In this also I think you will find more room for each person to apply it to himself." Not only is Mrs. Zendt made to conform, she is told, in effect, that this kind of conformity represents the real meaning of individuality; so she cannot object on either score. And, to nail it down, the service is simple; she had said she wanted simplicity; so if she does not find what she needs the fault is hers.

Of course we also note the cavalier way in which the meaning of baptism remains undiscussed. Pastor Zarvis, presumably with the intention of acknowledging Mrs. Zendt's individuality, fails utterly to convey to her anything about the function of the worshiping congregation in the ceremony of baptism. No doubt he believes he has liberal convictions. What he does is to convey the notion that baptism is a completely private affair. Thus the conformity into which he is unwittingly forcing Mrs. Zendt is one that lacks the combined sense of God and of the company of the faithful. At precisely the place where group relationship is fundamental, he dispenses with it. He wants action. He wants to get baptism and entrance into the church settled. He has no sense that he has done great disservice to Mrs. Zendt and her family—that he has, in effect, taught them the wrong way to approach the problems and potentialities of life.

Reconstructions are never certain. But let us, in any event, try to see what a different attitude on the part of the pastor could have meant in this situation:

MRS. ZENDT: I think that we have decided to have our little boy baptized in your church.

PASTOR: You mean the decision is almost made but that it hasn't been easy to get this far on it?

MRS. ZENDT: That's right. It has been difficult, although I guess our decision is as definite as we can make it. My husband and I have done a lot of thinking and discussing about it—not just about baptism but about religion in other ways too.

PASTOR: Then your present resolve has emerged out of serious thought and consideration?

MRS. ZENDT: Yes it has, although I'm not sure either my husband or I even now understand all the implications, and the possible complications. A lot of it has to do with the fact that I was brought up as a Catholic, and in a very strict way too.

PASTOR: That background is something, you mean, that you can't just put aside with one clean decision?

MRS. ZENDT: Yes, that's true. It does hang on, no matter what I do. But there's more than that as well.

This is perhaps enough to illustrate how very different the whole tone of the discussion could have been if the pastor had been genuinely alert to the subsurface concerns that were evident in every sentence Mrs. Zendt spoke. In terms of the content discussed, it might or might not have been different. What is different is that in the reconstructed interview the pastor permits nothing, not even his desire to get the baptism settled, to stand in the way of understanding the conflict from which Mrs. Zendt is emerging. From study of many situations of this type we know that such alertness to the negative as well as the positive dimension of her feelings will in the long run make her decision very much more sound and basic. That is another way of talking about just the kind of initiative that organization men forfeit. On occasion all this may delay a bit such decisions as the time of baptism or joining the church, but not necessarily. But always involved is helping people to mobilize, under God, the resources available to them, so that they learn, in the process of making *this* decision, how to proceed when confronted with the *next* situation. Unless this is done, we all become unwitting fosterers of the organization man, as ignorant of what we are doing as Pastor Zarvis was.

For the most part the discussion up to now has dealt with young adults. But I have implied that there is something about the busyness of the young adult's life that makes him look like an organization man even when he is not. This means very often that, however much he is an organization man, he is not so irremediably. Later on he may become such, in a way that is for all practical purposes irreversible.

So far as irreversibility is concerned therefore, the crucial point is likely to be reached in early middle age, which may come anywhere between thirty and forty-five. For the potentially irreversible organization man, middle age is reached when he begins to realize that, whatever it is that he is, he is stuck with it for the rest of his life—his kind of job, his place and mode of living, his children, his wife, his friends. If he accepts all this with no reflection, no conscious acknowledgment of inner boredom or meaninglessness or anxiety, then he will soon be irreversibly an organization man. If the idea of a second birth, even a very little birth, is not wholly foreign to him then there is hope.

As with the shepherding of young adults, the real task here is to avoid being so completely tied to the symptom or immediate problem that one fails to note the creative uneasiness that is trying to break through from underneath. A problem is a religious problem when it has religious dimensions, regardless of what it begins with—insomnia, drinking, adultery, marital quarreling, or what. In terms of method one does not, to be sure, say, "Don't take up my time with that insomnia stuff. I know your problem is deeper. Now come clean, brother." That is rejection. But knowing that every presented problem is a channel of access to something more basic can make us listen to the Thou in a way we would not otherwise do.

Conclusion

We began this discussion by noting five social analysts who have much in common in their understanding of trends toward conformity. We have used William Whyte's term but have dealt with the larger phenomenon. We analyzed first the trends toward conformity within the church and the ministry, and then turned to see similar trends in laymen, emphasizing the young adult group. At all points we have attempted to suggest the basic principles of Christian shepherding in relation to the people. Our desire is to help people move from heteronomous idolatry toward theonomy, with its implicit automony under God. We have tried to show ways in which shepherding may work for or against such an aim.

Let me close by returning to one of Whyte's pearls, and thus to our own first point—that we need first to acknowledge and deal with the subtle organization man trends in ourselves. Whyte quotes some advertising for the motion picture *A Man Called Peter*. This is attached to a photograph, he notes, of a man dressed very much like a junior executive, and the advertising reads in part as follows:

He was a first-name kind of guy. . . . He was everybody's kind of guy. . . . He unpomped the pompous, played baseball with kids, turned a two-hour leave into a honeymoon for a sailor and his girl, and gave voice to all the longings in a man's soul. . . . He was a lovin' kind of guy. . . . Every woman secretly had her eyes on him, but he had eyes for only one. . . . He was God's kind of guy.[8]

Whyte calls this profanity. Certainly it is blasphemy. It is heteronomous idolatry, and it is not wholly foreign, in its appeal, to any of us. With organization man, we begin from within.

VII. SHEPHERDING REBELS

In considering the shepherding of rebels, as in the previous chapter with conformists, we will do well to begin with some ecclesiastical self-examination. How, in fact, do we treat rebels in the ministry and in theological school? The answer to this question may reveal underlying attitudes that extend unconsciously to our shepherding of all rebels.

Ecclesiastical Rebels

Let us begin with some lower-case rebels in the person of theological students who have doubts about the faith or doubts about what the faith is represented to them to be by their teachers. In most denominational seminaries a generation or two ago, the area in which voiced doubt was permitted was relatively small and the area in which it was encouraged was smaller still. Has that situation changed? To a very considerable extent I believe it has changed. The conviction has increased that a student's honest wrestling with doubt may contain many positive elements, and that the faith with which he eventually emerges is likely to be far stronger than it would be if he had to keep the doubts to himself, or merely to share them with fellow doubters, but never with his teachers.

Most seminary teachers today will encourage a student to be honest about his doubts, regardless of their nature, provided they see within the person signs of honest and conscientious struggle with the issues involved. This is a great gain, and is founded on sound psychological principles. If doubt is unvoiced, or is shared only with brothers, but never with fathers, there will be trouble later on. Either the doubt will continue and fester, or the person will swing the pendulum and become a conformist. Active encouragement of doubt is, for a good many if not for all, an essential road to faith that is appropriated genuinely and inwardly. And on this our attitude improves all the time.

To be sure there are still worms in this basically solid apple. A student may be encouraged to deal openly with his doubt about almost everything except what a particular teacher, or school, regards as indispensable. And the definition of the indispensable comes in periods if not in fashions. In a past age the student might be stopped if he expressed doubt about a literal interpretation of the virgin birth or the literal inerrancy of Scripture. Today, with all our improvement, he might be discouraged for showing a preference for Paul Tillich as against Emil Brunner, or *vice versa,* depending on his school and his teacher. If he has doubts about the relevance of modern psychiatric findings to his work, he may be discouraged in some schools; and in others, he may be penalized if he regards these as important.

Another level of rebellion is found in those theological students who elect to attend interdenominational rather than denominational seminaries. At times this is mainly for pragmatic reasons, such as geographical proximity. At other times it is because a bright student believes, rightly or wrongly, that he will get better instruction. But often it is because such a student is rebelling against what he believes he will be confronted with in a denominational school by way of demand for conformity in belief or practice. I am not in any way here attempting to argue a case pro or con. For our purposes the question is: Does such a student run risks of not being accepted by his denomination? The answer, on a sheer statistical basis, is that the risks he runs are decreasing. This is due in part simply to the demand for ministers, and to the fact that the interdenominational schools are no longer regarded as hotbeds of heterodoxy. It is due largely, however, to the recognition that one person may be better able to move toward faith in one kind of environment than in another. Here too there seem to be real gains.

I am impressed also that theological students involved in various kinds of moral rebelliousness are handled somewhat differently than in past periods. Whatever may be the final decision in such a case, it is now a rare school that does not seek first to find out something about the specific motivations for the behavior, and in this way to help the person whether he is to remain in the school or not. For example, it may indeed be necessary that a man who is discovered engaging in homosexual behavior be prevented from entering the ministry. But the first question is what kind of help is needed to aid him to work through the undoubted distortions that have led to this behavior. If such help is found and pursued, he may emerge a strong man and effective minister. If not, then he should be barred, but it is immensely important that the first effort come first. I have been encouraged by the increased understanding of things of this sort, both in theological schools and in the church judicatories. Much remains to be done, but the direction is right.

There is another dimension of all this, however, about which I am less happy. This can be illustrated by reference to my own field. When courses in clinical pastoral training were begun a generation ago, the students who participated in them generally did so without strong moral blessing from their churches or theological schools. They were sometimes warned against the dangers of psychiatry, or admonished not to become too much enamored of counseling. Generally they were regarded as rebels, and in a sense many of them were. Having lived through that period, I know that some such students felt themselves confronted by a mass of theory much of which seemed to them irrelevant, while the actual direct work with people seemed both attractive and relevant. This was of course before the biblical and theological revival of today had made such a dichotomy difficult. Today we do not have the same degree of suspiciousness of a generation ago, but it is not gone.

I would be the first to say that work in this field should have a theological and a pastoral perspective, and not that of psychiatry, social work, or other disciplines. Further, we need to scrutinize steadily the often unstated assumptions held by many persons in such related areas. Yet we have much to learn from them. If a student, in the flush of such learning, turns in temporary rebellion against something else, our task would appear to be encouraging him to move on until he sees the theological dimensions in what has caught his imagination, not in discouraging him from such exploration at all. This can hardly be done unless his school takes this exploration seriously, and no longer regards this field as something that can be done by somebody's left hand on Saturday mornings. This kind of interest is gaining in popularity. If not properly cultivated, we run the risk of making permanent rebels out of persons who, with the right kind of teaching in relation to their interest, can move by this interest to deeper apprehension and assimilation of the faith itself.

Finally, in our consideration of attitudes exercised toward ministers and theological students, have we penalized the rebel with creative ideas by refusing to give him a position of leadership? By any standards, the church record on this point seems mixed. Most positions of leadership are given, in the church as elsewhere, to men who lie somewhere between unquestioning loyalty to the organization and capacity for creative innovation. Mere conformists are generally capable of leadership only in the lower echelons, and rebels who are too far in left field plainly cannot be trusted to identify with organizational interests. The question, then, is largely one of degree. To my eye, the offices regarded as highest seem too often to be given to men whose loyalty is more obvious than their creativity. While it is now improving, the administrative leadership of our theological schools has too rarely been given to men who have creative ideas about education, and who have the background to support those ideas.

The greatest danger we run today is in relation to the young and creative rebel whose concern contains sound elements, but who will have to transform and deepen it through some experiential fires. If his concern is prophetic, he will have to learn that he can speak prophetically and be heard and heeded by his people only if he first builds up a relationship with them. If his concern is intellectual, he will need to discover that the intellectual essentials can usually be stated understandably, and that technicality and profundity are not always co-ordinate. If his concern is pastoral, he will have to learn that this cannot absolve him from operating in a representative role which, on occasion, demands toughness. Whatever the thrust of his creativity, he will have to learn to channel it within a total context. But only harm can result if the creativity itself is repressed or shunted aside or made to appear wholly unacceptable.

There is another way in which we can see the larger danger in dealing with rebels. This is that we tend to accept or reject a man wholly on the basis of the *content* of his rebellion, judged from our own point of view, and not also in terms of what the rebellion, inwardly, means to him. The human mind is complex, and we cannot automatically and easily tell what this inward meaning is. We may believe we know when we do not, and as a result encourage one form of rebellion because its surface content looks sound, and discourage another, because it does not—with the possibility of being wrong in both instances.

Shepherding of the rebel, regardless of the content his rebellion assumes, should begin with exploration of its meaning to him. This does not mean that we set aside objective considerations. We do, however, attempt to prevent them from acting as barriers to inner comprehension. Whether the rebellion turns out to be genuine creativeness trying to break through, or iconoclasm based on inner weakness, we cannot possibly help the person who has it unless we begin by trying to grasp its meaning for him.

It is my contention that these principles we have reached by a brief examination of rebels in the ministry supply us with the basic clues to our general shepherding of rebels.

Lay Rebels

Recently Philip E. Jacob published a report describing and evaluating the findings of several recent studies about attitudes and values in college students. Jacob's own conclusion is that a very high percentage of students are out-and-out conformists. I want to question some aspects of this conclusion, but let us first get something of Jacob's view in his own words:

A dominant characteristic of students in the current generation is that they are *gloriously contented* both in regard to their present day-to-day activity and their outlook for the future. Few of them are worried—about their health, their prospective careers, their family relations, the state of national or international society or the likelihood of their enjoying secure and happy lives. They are supremely confident that their destinies lie within their own control rather than in the grip of external circumstances.

The great majority of students appear unabashedly *self-centered*. They aspire for material gratifications for themselves and their families. They intend to look out for themselves first and expect others to do likewise.

But this is not the individualistic self-centeredness of the pioneer. American students fully accept the conventions of the contemporary business society as the context within which they will realize their personal desires. They cheerfully expect to conform to the economic status quo and to receive ample rewards for dutiful and productive effort.

Social harmony with an *easy tolerance of diversity* pervades the student environment. Conformists themselves, the American students see little need to insist that each and every person be and behave just like themselves.

The traditional *moral virtues are valued* by almost all students. They respect sincerity, honesty, loyalty, as proper standards of conduct for decent people. But they are not inclined to censor those who choose to depart from these canons.

Students normally express a *need for religion* as a part of their lives and make time on most weekends for an hour in church. But there is a "ghostly quality" about the beliefs and practices of many

119

of them. . . . Their religion does not carry over to guide and govern important decisions in the secular world. Students expect these to be socially determined. God has little to do with the behavior of men in society, if widespread student judgment be accepted. His place is in church and perhaps in the home, not in business or club or community. He is worshipped, dutifully and with propriety, but the campus is not permeated by a live sense of His presence.[1]

If there is truth at all, as I believe there is, in Jacob's picture of a majority of contemporary college students, that truth lies less in depiction of the student as a breed unto himself and more in a general image of adults in our society. There are unique elements about the college population, but those are not what I plan to lift up here for comment.

Let us grant the truth in Jacob's case, which is a form of the organization-man hypothesis. I am then impressed by two things. The first is that we may be getting this result by rewarding conformity or by penalizing creativity whenever it looks like rebellion. Even if there are large numbers of people who are conformists, part of the reason for that may be that they never had help when creativity and individuality threatened to break through the conformist patterns.

The other point is that, in my own observation, there is a great deal of external conformity that covers over an inner and unacknowledged rebellion. This rebellion, in which there is much latent creativity, apparently tends to suffer so many penalties if brought into the open that many people handle the problem by ignoring it altogether.

If we simply take the conformist hypothesis, how can we account, for example, for the rising rate of juvenile delinquency? At first glance these two points seem to be in contradiction. Be assured that I have no new light to shed on the delinquency problem. The causes are certainly complex, but I would suggest as one of them that the way of the rebel is now being made so hard that if one adheres to it, he must do so at great cost, and is therefore likely to overdo whatever the impulsions were that first made him a rebel. Of course I am aware also of the conformity to a gang that is often found in delinquency.

My general conclusion is that the way of the rebel has been made so difficult that he is likely either to abandon the creativity imbedded in his rebellion, or else to overdo its expression in ways that are unconstructive and bring penalties upon him. If this is so, then the question of shepherding the rebel is not merely one of dealing with him once his rebelliousness has become open, but is also one of encouraging him to confront and deal with tendencies in himself he had not dared to admit were his.

With the rebel, then, we have two kinds of tasks. If his rebellion is in the open, then our attempt is to aid him to build upon the creative or constructive aspect of his rebellion and gradually to set aside the hostile or aggressive or iconoclastic aspects. If his rebellion is concealed, then our effort is to help him to bring it out in trust that with help from our sympathetic understanding, its creative aspects may be so channeled by him that he will not be unduly penalized but will become productive.

The psychology of shepherding the rebel is also, at the same time, the psychology of most evangelism, provided the evangelistic situation is properly understood. If a person not in the faith accepted fully, positively, and quickly whatever we had to say about the faith, then he would either have moved into the faith already, needing only our confirmatory words, or else he would be a conformist. Real evangelism is helping someone to relate the faith to himself and his needs and to truth in a way he had not done before. No doubt there are still many places in the world where this means bringing the hitherto unheard Word to the person. But in a culture like ours everybody has heard some kind of word. For various reasons it has not been accepted. Technically, then, such a person is more rebel than ignorant.

Let us look in briefly on two or three pastoral contacts. In the first Pastor A is making a call at the home of the Abels, and the door has been answered by Mr. Abel, who had signed the church guest register a couple of weeks previously:

PASTOR A: I am Pastor A of Blank Church. I noticed that you had attended our church recently, and wanted to say hello to you and your family and invite you to come into our fellowship—if you are not already a member of a local church.

MR. ABEL: Well, it's nice of you to drop by. I don't know about joining your church. It's pretty and all, but it's mighty big and it did seem kind of—well, cold.

PASTOR A: But our people are really very warm. Just wait until you get inside, and you'll see how they will really welcome you.

MR. ABEL: Well, sir, that may be so and all, but I don't know as my family and I could ever feel at home in such a big place. You see, we came from Smalltown, and . . .

PASTOR A: Why, half our people are from little towns and rural areas too. And I want to assure you that nowhere in America will you find a warmer quality of fellowship than we have.

(P.S. He didn't make the sale.) If this is caricature, remember that it merely exaggerates what may go on every day in

122

slightly less extreme form, and by such small things people can be led farther away.

Here is another situation. In a young people's meeting a college student, Bob, has blurted out in a discussion of conscience that he understands from social science that conscience is nothing but a reflection of the culture and does not, therefore, have the holy meaning that religion seems to give to it. At the close of the meeting Pastor B has walked over to Bob; and when the others leave, they fall into conversation:

PASTOR B: I gathered, Bob, that you felt a lot of the discussion of conscience was on the wrong foot?

BOB: Yes, I did. Of course I'm not too sure about it, but it seems that our consciences just reflect what we've been taught, and maybe that's right and maybe it isn't.

PASTOR B: That's right, Bob, and that's just what modern theology holds. Conscience can be a very deceptive instrument, taking us away from proper reliance on God's grace and the church. Why, just last week I was reading Brunner on conscience. If you think you're suspicious of it, you ought to read him. Now I just happen to have his book in my hip pocket. Sit down there and let me read this to you. I'm sure this will straighten you out.

In answering a question that Bob has not asked, the pastor is of course impressing Bob with irrelevancy. What the pastor is getting at may indeed be true, but it will obviously leave Bob confused. Suppose we back up and ask what Pastor B might have done at the crucial point where he went astray:

PASTOR B: That is, as you see it conscience is a mirror of our rearing, and in itself is not a guarantee of the rightness or wrongness of what is said?

123

Bob: Yes, that's it. But religion says that conscience is the voice of God.

Pastor B: If it's relative and fallible, then how can it be the voice of God without making God into something relative and fallible?

Bob: Yes, that's right. What is the answer to that, sir?

Pastor B: It seems to me you have drawn a perfectly logical conclusion from your premises, Bob. If both the premises are correct, then what you say certainly follows.

Bob: But you've already said you agreed that the content of conscience does depend on culture.

Pastor B: Right. But I did not say that conscience is the voice of God.

Bob: You mean religion doesn't say that? Why, I had always thought . . .

There would seem an excellent chance that Bob will get help in clarifying his understanding of conscience. And note that, in doing this, the pastor does not need to hesitate in helping Bob to get an idea clarified. But he first sees what Bob's assumptions are. What he says is relevant to Bob's understanding.

It is my conviction that an immense number of evangelistic opportunities is lost because of discussions of precisely this kind. We tend to identify ourselves as answer men. Under the mistaken impression that an answer on our lips will meet a question in the other person, we give it; and very often it is irrelevant to the way this person feels or thinks, because we have not examined the situation first from his point of view. If, as is often true, his problem is not mere misapprehension, as in Bob, but is also a deeper antagonism, we run even greater danger of alienating him still more from the gospel.

The real answer to this dilemma seems to me to lie in

our theology itself. If we are in the faith, conscious of the transformation it has wrought upon us despite the unlikeliness of the material it has had to work with, we are aware that, whatever has happened, we have not "arrived." We cannot, then, identify ourselves with faith as an achievement in such a way that we have lost contact with doubt, or rebelliousness, or negativity and question. If what we have is, in the deepest sense, a gift, then we can identify with the struggles of someone else just as much as we can with his assimilation of faith. Knowing that his rebellion may be, in the providence of God, a necessary step in his move to the faith, we can give attention to him in the struggle and the process, and not just to a hypothetical person who has moved far beyond and is in the faith. We become direction-minded rather than end-pointed.

Only in this way, I think, can our shepherding of rebels be true Christian shepherding. If we have not some trace of rebel in us, then we deceive ourselves, or we have become mere conformists. But if we have, and acknowledge this, the very ability to do so betokens our recognition that our faith too has been a gift of grace. We can then help the rebel without being defensive about our loyalty. We can help the doubter without losing our faith.

Finally, I believe that much we confront today that looks like indifference to religion is actually, if we can get to it, rebelliousness. It is a kind of passive, fence-sitting declaration of the irrelevance of religion. The very metaphor of fence-sitting should give us the clue. Fences are not easy seats. People choose them only when something in themselves cannot wholly give up the notion that there just might be something worth while on the other side of the fence. At this point much of our testimony about the faith to the apparently indifferent requires criticism. Sometimes we need to demonstrate relevance not only, or even at all, with our lips, but in our lives and our service. Few of the indifferent are such from mere laziness. Theirs is a resistance, albeit of a passive type. Seldom can they be fast-talked out of indifference. Here also, shepherding may begin with the establishment of relevance.

Conclusion

In my repeated injunction to find out what the rebel's rebelliousness means to him, I am far from asserting that all rebellion is of the same order. But an astonishing lot of rebellion is potential creativity. And how, until we try, can we assert it is not? If it is not, we may be serpents. But until that is clear, we had better be doves.

VIII. SHEPHERDING HOUSEWIVES

Recently I taught a special evening course for the wives of students in the Federation of Theological Schools at The University of Chicago. The topic was selected by the wives—self-understanding through psychology and religion.

At the third session I asked the wives to write me anonymous questions, areas, problems, or situations they would like me to discuss in the course of the other sessions. About fifty questions were received, and they proved so interesting that I devoted all the remaining sessions to discussing them directly.

This was certainly not a typical group of housewives, if indeed there is such anywhere. Person for person, they were surely more intelligent than any mere cross-section would be. Perhaps as many as half of them were wives of students doing work beyond the B.D. degree which, at least in this group, implied more than the usual degree of commitment to help a husband get where he believes he should go. At least most of them, as represented by their attendance at this course on some nights with very bad weather, as well as in many of their questions, must have had a positive view of the Christian faith over and above their identification with it through their husbands. Their average age would certainly be greater than that of a group of wives in a school training only for the B.D. degree; but as a group, they were still in the twenties.

What struck me, in examining their anonymous questions,

was that the unusual character of the questions and situations could shed light on more typical housewife problems in a way that would be difficult to get at through more typical housewives. Let me give a few of their questions.

One wife wrote:

I would like very much to have you discuss the goals that might be achieved—the possible values derived—from a student's wife's years here in this setting, and her involvement in more of this process than merely earning the family income.

This grows out of my concern at the attitude expressed last fall by several wives of faculty members, at a joint meeting, that husbands do not want their wives to be involved in what they are doing or thinking about, or in their religious and intellectual development.

This is such a complete contradiction, it seems to me, to the kind of thing our former dean of students kept saying to wives' groups in recent years. He spoke always of this kind of educational process as involving all of life, and about the real need for wives to grow along with their husbands. Which position is right?

Criteria for Wives

The preceding seems to me a very perceptive and a very difficult question. An intelligent young wife has believed that she should attempt to grow with her husband. But she has encountered a group of faculty wives who pass on the worldly wisdom that she will really do better to keep away from her husband's work. What does she do? If she now tries to keep up in some way with her husband, she will suspect herself of meddling. But if she does not, then she believes in principle that she is in the same position as the suburban wife of an insurance man. Note carefully that the question is not about what the minister's wife should do

128

in the church. The dangers of the dominating or ambitious wife are too well known to need comment, and we know that almost everywhere ministers' wives are given more of the privileges of individuality than ever before. The question is about the intellectual and spiritual relationship between the husband's interests and those of his wife.

Any flat answer to the question can be dangerous. If we say, for instance, that religion is different, and of course a wife should follow her husband, and thus be different from the insurance man, does that mean she becomes a pseudo-professional without professional education? Does she really have to know that Barth puts Christ before Adam, that the "filioque" clause prevented the separation of transcendence from immanence, or what *The Christian Century* was against last week?

If we say, on the other hand, that she should be a wife like any other wife, and let her husband go about his profession as a lawyer's wife lets her husband go about his, does that imply that the proper norm for husbands and wives is to separate home and occupation categorically? Is the concept of Christian vocation so absolutely individual that it has nothing at all to say to a family? Or must intellectual growth, for either husband or wife, be confined to hi-fi sets and the book of the month, and wholly separated from the husband's professional concerns?

We must of course concede that some of the interest the young wife has in keeping up with her husband is probably romantic in nature. Since he seems to eat, drink, and sleep Niebuhr, Paul, or Calvin, she had best do so too unless she wants to be starved. When the romantic flush is past, she may be able to distinguish those aspects of her husband's interests that are technical from those that are general and continue to follow the second, while reserving the right to remain ignorant of the first. Right now that distinction may be too difficult to make. Perhaps it is the distinction the faculty wives were trying to make. For their sake, I hope it was. The plain danger is that the baby will get thrown out with the bath—Barth's basic point of view will be ejected along with the technical material, and religion for the wife, apart from conformist churchgoing, will become just what insurance is for the insurance man's wife. If she looks for any intellectual interests, she will look anywhere else but to religious sources.

Let us suppose that she now invests her mind completely in her husband's interest, technicalities and all. Disillusionment is certain. Someday she must decide between reading the new Bultmann book and bathing the baby. She may thereafter feel frustrated, condemned to drudgery, divorced from intellectual life—because she failed to distinguish the essential from the technical. In addition, she may fail to use her mind on what she is doing—beginning with babies —and thus not help her husband's mind to grow in areas where it ought to be growing—again beginning with babies.

Let us suppose, on the other hand, that she decides right off that she will not attempt to follow her husband's interest. She wants to be just a housewife, she may say. This may appeal to her husband's virility. When he quotes a Greek verb now and then, she may look at him in admiration like the wife of the hero of the World Series or the wife of the physicist who has just split an atom. Incidentally, this is bad for her husband. He may indeed have hair on his chest. But his wife unfortunately is teaching him that men are really the human beings who count and that women, although they may be useful, and even precious to God and man, really do not possess much above the ears. For a man who will be ministering, on the average, to about two women for every one man, this seems to be getting off to a bad start.

Here was another wife's question: "My husband is in the process of 'finding himself.' Consequently he is changing. Most of the changes are improvements, but some are irritating, and on rare occasions he seems somewhat like a stranger." Let us assume, as does the wife, that the changes in her husband are in the direction of deepening his faith and his understanding. Still, she finds some of them irritating and even, on occasion, alienating. It may be that her husband is simply going through a period in which he is taking himself too seriously. Even so, that may be a part of his intellectual and spiritual development. The real question being asked by the wife is this: If my husband does grow intellectually and spiritually, will this fact increasingly alienate him from me? How can I prevent his development from isolating us?

Some of the wives' questions revealed more about specific types of problems they are confronting. For instance, one wrote: "How can one accept himself when he realizes his lack of concern for others, his lack of a sincere interest for things of the spirit, rebellion against intellectual matters, and when he realizes his own self-centeredness?"

Another wrote: "How is one able to express the inner thoughts or ideas that haunt his mind and make him have guilty feelings? When one is reluctant to talk about these things, and can't because of embarrassment or some such attitude, how can he come willingly to talk about it so as to understand the fact and to help understand his present state?"

Still another asked: "Many times I have a feeling that the other person is better than I, and I become disturbed by it. What can I do to prove to myself that I am just as good as the other person?"

Some of the questions were about children, since many of the wives were also mothers. Here is one: "Why is it that the traits and idiosyncrasies which we despised and literally fought so much in our parents are the same ones which we now find apparent in our own living? How can we deal with this problem—should we try to reconcile and analyze these 'bad' traits as inherent and not as bad as we first thought, or should we try to fight to rid ourselves of them?"

There are many more interesting questions on my list. But piling up too many could obscure the point for which they are being introduced. That point is this: So long as these wives can keep themselves sensitively open enough to ask questions like this seriously, they are continuing to engage in the concrete processes of spiritual and intellectual growth. So long as they ask the questions, the answers they find may be more or less satisfying to them. They may have to alter some of the questions before they can find answers at all, but the danger will come when questions are no longer asked.

Our general subject is the Christian shepherding of housewives. The first basic point that can be made is this: The housewife who is still asking serious and basic questions about her intellectual and spiritual development, and its relation to her husband's, can always be helped. The wife who has no questions either does not need shepherding, or else is unprepared to receive it. I began by saying that the group of wives of theological students was untypical, and yet that their questions could shed light on more typical situations. This is so, I believe, because it is my impression that a very large number of housewives are today asking basic questions—even though they may be less articulate and less well-informed than the theological students' wives, and even though their questions may be less direct and more concealed.

Wives Young, Middle, and Older

I have no new information nor fresh wisdom about the place of the housewife in our society, but a few things are fairly obvious. The first is that there are more housewives, absolutely and proportionately. On the average, more women marry, and marry younger; and the high birth rate shows that most of them begin to have children very soon. The second is that the social prestige attached to being a housewife has increased in recent years. There is a good deal of evidence that most women who are gainfully employed outside the home do so mainly from economic necessity. This contrasts with the attitude in the earlier days of the modern movement for the emancipation of women.

There is a good deal of talk about the way in which labor-saving devices free the housewife, and of course in some respects they do. But in a young married woman's life most of this time won from laundry and weaving is devoted to more concentrated attention on children. There is some genuine relief from physical effort, but a good part of the energy saved is plowed back into house, husband, and children. Since more and more housewives are in the middle class, and more and more are entering the upper middle class, the pattern of ambition characteristic of that class affects more wives. There is, for instance, more effort to

133

see that young children are socializing properly, and consequently more worry when the proper standards of socializing are not being met.

The picture I have of an increasing number of housewives is not of a beautifully gowned young mother sipping a cup of tea in a spotless kitchen that practically cleans itself, but of a slightly messy young woman in slacks trying to persuade a child to eat his breakfast, or on the telephone asking if the repair man can come look at the broken dishwasher before next Wednesday. Relief from old forms of backbreaking labor there may indeed be. But the housewife and mother of young children still has a twenty-four hour a day job.

Let us look at this young housewife in church. She is certainly to be found there in increasing numbers. Because of viruses, and sometimes Saturday night parties, she is not regular in her church attendance; but she does pretty well. An offhand question to her about the meaning of religion would often draw the remark that church is good for the children and for the family. Her time, her energy, and her interests are so family involved that she may often appear to be quite unlike the wives of the theological students.

Even with her I think such a conclusion is deceptive. If we give her a chance, she will often come up with very searching questions, especially about religious development in children. The most important fact about her religious life, however, is that, with all her busyness, she is presumably building up a relationship to religion and the church against the day of special need. Right now the questions she has may be unvoiced. But even if they are not, her apparently passive church participation ought not to be regarded merely as negative. Needless to say, where the vitality and imagination of a church program also help to make her articulate during this busy period, the gain is far greater. We can note especially that any particular individual or family problem of this period on which she seeks help is important not only in itself, but also in cementing her relationship to the faith and the church.

The larger problem of shepherding the housewife seems to me to come after the period of young adulthood. More than a generation ago Carl Jung declared that there is a crisis of middle years, by which he did not mean that life begins at forty.[1] He believes that this crisis is essentially spiritual in nature. Here is the general line of argument. In young adulthood there is inevitably a kind of extraverted period. Husbands are getting on with their jobs; wives are getting on with their children; everybody is thoroughly occupied—so occupied that the question of life's meaning tends to be answered by activity before it is asked. But there comes a time when activity alone is not the answer. Either some goals are achieved, or they never will be. If achieved, they may appear less valuable in reality than they did in anticipation. If not achieved, they may give a sense of helplessness.

Jung has no intention of stopping activity. He believes there must be a consciously recognized movement inward if middle years are to be fruitful, while this has been less necessary in the young adult years. If there is basic reconsideration, reassessment of goals to give more value to inward affairs, then life may move ahead at a deeper level than before. If this is resisted, then new forms of difficulty arise.

Let us not be thrown off the scent of the basic situation

135

by preoccupation with externals. For instance, it is often said that a woman confronts this crisis when her last child leaves home for the adult world. This may indeed symbolize a completion of the move into the new condition, but it is only the last spike. The process has been going on for some time. Similarly, it is not enough to say that one should acquire hobbies or other interests, valuable as they may be. According to Jung, no interests and activities of an external kind will suffice unless there is first a spiritual rebirth. And even Jung does not minimize how difficult this is.

I am impressed that a very high proportion of difficulties —illnesses, alcoholism—reach their statistical peak in the late thirties and early forties. Whatever the individual forces behind them, I believe this suggests also a general failure to confront the new task of reassessment that might have been done before, but which at this stage becomes mandatory. By whatever terms we call it, this process will have painful elements. Let us not minimize these, nor believe it can be brought about by a few well chosen words.

We have stressed Jung's view that this crisis of middle years must focus around an inner reconsideration. This says important things about the relative openness to such rebirth on the part of men and women. For the most part, our culture associates inwardness with femininity. It is a good deal more difficult for the average man to confront his inwardness than for the woman, because culture puts extra barriers before the man. Even so it can hardly be said to be easier for the woman. But she does confront fewer artificial hurdles.

There is hardly a church where the pastor could deny that he is consulted by more women than men in their thirties. This is not necessarily because women have more or deeper problems, be they housewives or single. It is mainly because women, with a bit of help, can confront the inward dimension of their situation with less inhibition than men. We could say too that men find it harder to accept the reality of their dependency needs than do women. It is immensely important that the pastor understand this. Otherwise, because more women consult him than men, he may find himself believing that women have more problems, are inherently weaker, and do not have the staying power of men. It is most dubious that any of these things is true.

When we move on into late middle years, there will be a decisive difference depending on how the woman has negotiated the crisis of early middle life. For her who has done so, these years may well be the richest of all in terms both of fulfillment and of service, and of the relationship between them. But if the meeting of that crisis is still unfinished business, then the woman in late middle years may confront even greater spiritual dangers than her husband, for he has an investment in work and occupation which, if nothing else, keeps him active and alert. For the wife one form of this is the humorous futility that Helen Hokinson used to depict in her cartoons. It is not always so funny.

When we reach the older years, there is one fact of immense importance, that women tend to outlive men, on the average, by about five years. And wives are apparently the most long-lived of women. The average housewife must, then, in sheer prudence, contemplate spending the last five years of her life without her husband. Of all the groups that may seem most foreign to the young minister, old ladies generally head the list. Yet if ever Christian shepherding is needed, that is the time.

Problems and Potentialities

There are many special problems possessed by some groups of housewives that need to be considered in a general account. Perhaps the most important is the women who are childless against their own wish. Inability to conceive is of course often due to the husband, and the first move should always be a medical examination of both husband and wife. What should be recognized is the deep sense of inadequacy a wife may feel when she is unable to conceive, even when this results from nothing she herself could have controlled. Sometimes equally deep-reaching is the problem of the wife on whom surgery has been performed which prevents her having children, or having more children. Since we ministers are mostly men, we cannot fully appreciate what such things mean to a woman. So it is that, feeling inadequate and even embarrassed, we often try to slide too quickly to a "solution" of a problem like this, without really performing the first function of shepherding, namely, listening until we really grasp the other person's feeling.

One final point needs to be made, although it has been implied in what has gone before. We have noted that the culture puts fewer barriers before a woman in examining internal matters. Other things being equal, this means that women as a group may be more likely than men to approach the Christian faith through what is, in a very general sense, a psychological point of view. Without asserting in any way that there is complete harmony between psychology and theology, I would nevertheless state that a minister who had not done some psychological exploration would confront special handicaps in his ministry to women in general, and to housewives in particular.

138

Let me close with a thoughtful question from one of my theological student wives.

Do you believe that the modern psychological approach toward self-understanding is a servant to the Christian faith, or a substitute for the Christian faith?

The reason I ask this is because I get the impression from some persons that they have a tendency to make an either-or choice, and they are not sure which side to accept, the traditional or the modern. There seems to be a difficulty relating the traditional to the modern view. There is a tendency to throw overboard the traditional views of the Christian faith and to say that all the answers to our existence and personal problems can be reached apart from Christ.

Personally, I believe that modern psychology, philosophy, and other fields can help us to understand better our relationship to God, God's relationship to us, as well as our relationship to other people as revealed by Christ. I believe these fields of knowledge can be our servants, and we need not reject Christ and his message of hope. Have I radically misunderstood you, to believe that you hold a similar position? That you believe it is possible to relate the present views to the past views?

I feel no qualms in attempting to understand myself in the light of present psychological methods and findings, and yet I still relate these findings to Christ and his message of compassion, love, repentance, and hope. Can the modern approach complement the traditional view or must we accept one and reject the other?

This wife had certainly caught the spirit of what I had been trying to convey to the group. But note her suggestion that strong forces pull her and other wives in one direction or the other. There could be a certain economy of psychic effort in believing that everything is already to be found in the tradition, ignoring the fact that the tradition too had a psychological dimension requiring critical examination.

Conversely there could be psychic economy in settling for what seems new and psychological, and rejecting the traditional and theological as remote, forgetting that not infrequently theological questions are masked under psychological clothing.

Perhaps especially for women but not exclusively, the very penetration in modern psychology and psychiatry could lead them to think that is the sufficient path unto salvation. In my judgment, the one effective way to prevent this unfortunate result is to incorporate the real findings and methods into theological theory and pastoral operation, genuinely assimilating whatever is true and useful. If we scorn it altogether, we are both poor apologists for the faith and poor shepherds to the needs of men and women.

IX. SHEPHERDING THROUGH FELLOWSHIP

In one of the concluding paragraphs of his great book *A History of the Cure of Souls,* John T. McNeill writes:

The idea that every Christian is a priest toward his neighbor was one of the most vivid doctrines of the Reformation. Luther stressed the possibilities of spiritual enrichment by mutual edification. Bucer and Calvin gave the principle some organizational setting. It was stressed in Spener's writings and practiced in the Pietist movement of which he was the principal founder, and was given great prominence in its Moravian branch. John Wesley seized upon it, and its use in early Methodism was remarkably active, both for "edification" and for "correction." In our busy times a similar use of it would be difficult to secure. Yet, it appears in innumerable group movements, retreats, and enthusiastic sects, and people seem inclined to practice it where opportunity is given. "Where two or three are gathered together," it is always possible. But in mutual reproof and correction a marked difference arises with regard to whether the number is two or more. Two persons do not succeed very well, ordinarily, in correcting each other. It was natural that this mutual discipline should have been practiced mainly in groups rather than in pairs. No doubt a great deal of it goes on without the participants being aware that they are engaged in a traditionally honored practice. Like all methods of soul guidance, it is subject to abuses and deterioration, but a well-guarded use of mutual lay guidance would probably prove very valuable, relieving troubled consciences and toning up many feeble souls. It has its scientific counterpart in modern experimental methods of group psychotherapy.[1]

The constructive suggestion that there is more to be followed up in the "mutual care of souls" than has yet been done is especially interesting coming from John Mc-Neill. Although his historical expositions are detailed and without fault, his practical and constructive applications are made only when he feels genuine conviction.

Our main thesis will be precisely the same as McNeill's, namely, that far more shepherding can be done mutually than we have yet realized. But while agreeing with him on the main issue, and on the potential significance of group therapy and group dynamics for Christian shepherding, we shall have to raise questions about some of his other points. In our meaning, shepherding does not involve "discipline" in the ordinary sense, which is also the sense in which McNeill speaks of it here. In that usual sense, discipline is the group's or organization's dealing with someone who has offended in a specific fashion. It does not imply that everyone is at the same time doing something to or with everybody else. As we have already indicated, "discipline" in this ordinary sense cannot be considered irrelevant to the operations of the church. In our definition, however, this is relegated to another rubric of the work of the church than shepherding.

Along with this we need to raise a question about the meaning of "edification" and "correction," and of the relationship between them. If "correction" refers to the reproof of one offender by several other persons, then it belongs to discipline and is not part of shepherding. If edification carries the connotation merely of positive support, then we shall have to assert that this is a goal of fellowship, but not an accurate representation of movement toward it.

142

McNeill's statement that it makes a difference whether the number gathered together is two, or more than two, is an acute observation. His conclusion that things are easier with three or more is true only of discipline as he uses the term. When it comes to shepherding, only this statement can be true: For some people in some situations, shepherding is impeded if there are more than two; but with other people in other situations, shepherding can get under way only if there are more than two.

Group Process and Task

In the best chapter of his recent book entitled *Counseling and Theology,* William E. Hulme notes that the theological reason why a Protestant must help another to help himself instead of trying to do the helping in his stead is that we show belief in universal priesthood only if we attempt at all times to enhance the priestly potential of the other.[2] To give him answers, instead of helping him to work toward them, is an implicit denial of the other's priesthood capacity. Hulme's reference is to one-to-one relationships, but the same is true of groups.

In my judgment, the modern studies that go under such titles as "group dynamics," "group therapy," or "democratic group leadership," have discovered one fact of supreme importance about the inner workings of group life. Other discoveries, some of which we shall note presently, are also significant, but this one heads the hierarchy. It is this: The key to effective group operation is the proper handling of negative feelings. So stated, we recall at once that this is also a cardinal principle in one-to-one shepherding relationships. What does it mean in the group context?

Suppose we consider a hypothetical group of some six or

eight persons. Like most groups, this one has some task to perform. Jones opens the meeting, "Personally, I'm all for it; let's buy new pew cushions for the left chancel." Brown is next, "Jones is certainly right, and I go him one better and propose we get them for the right chancel too." Jones then agrees. Smith says, "You men are really correct, and I agree, and in addition propose them for the left front balcony." Jones and Brown agree. Green then puts in for the right front balcony; Miller for the left rear balcony; Johnson for the right rear balcony; and so it goes. My guess is that no one would recognize this meeting, because no group of human beings operates this way. This is hypothetical for the good reason that it never happened; or, if it did, it was because the parson rigged the meeting before it opened.

A very much more likely account of such a meeting would go like this:

JONES: I understand we're supposed to be a committee to consider new pew cushions. Personally, I don't know what the board had in mind. They ought to know we haven't got that new furnace paid for yet.

BROWN: And we only unloaded that roofing bill a few months ago.

SMITH: O.K., O.K. But those cushions on the left side of the chancel, especially in the first row, do look ratty. I heard the bishop mentioned them to Mrs. Goldbricks when he was here last month.

JONES: Well, if the bishop doesn't like them, get him to shake the dough for new ones out of Mrs. Goldbricks.

SMITH: Sure, that would be fine, but you know even the bishop wouldn't have much chance there. The thing you fellows are forgetting is how those cushions look from about ten rows in front. Why, just last Sunday . . .

GREEN: (*Interrupting*) I'm sorry to break in, but it hurts me to see this important matter put on so crass a basis. The real question is: What would the Lord want us to do?

Perhaps this account is caricature, but there are likely to be few who cannot find in it resemblances to meetings, living and dead, in which they have participated. Consider how many negative feelings were expressed in so short a time. Jones was negative about the board's action in referring the matter without remembering the furnace. Brown was negative on the same count plus the roofing bill. Smith felt negative because the church did not live up to the bishop's expectations. Jones was negative against bishops who tell what should be done and do not help do it. Green was negative because the discussion was too prudential and not on the basis of higher things. No doubt in a real meeting the negativities would be expressed more cautiously, but they would be there. Indeed, the very fact that they are expressed so readily gives some indication that there is more trust within the group than the content alone would suggest.

Let us be clear that a mere *expression* of negativities is not enough. Instead, something has to be done with them. Let us assume that Jones has made his opening statement, inveighing against the board's referring the matter while the bill for the new furnace is still unpaid. Suppose that Brown, instead of having his mind wholly on the roofing and furnace bills, is paying some attention to Jones, and says, "Does that mean, Jones, that if you saw some way to get these cushions without the church having a dangerous financial load, you might be for some such plan as this?" Jones may reply with an affirmative, qualified or unqualified. In that event, everyone recognizes that Jones will go along with the plan on certain conditions. Or Jones may answer that that is not the whole basis of his objection. He may want to retain the old cushions because they were a gift from his great-grandfather, or he may hate music and want the choir to be uncomfortable. In that case, the rest of the group will understand better what Jones's feelings are and will be able to deal with them in the open.

In its simplest form, this effort by Brown to pay attention to what Jones means and to get him to clarify it portrays the effective way of dealing with negative feelings. This attention-paying, clarifying function may be performed by one who is thought of as the leader, or by anyone else. What is meant, above all else, by the ambiguous phrase "group-centered leadership," is what happens in a group in which any member feels equally free and equally concerned to help another to clarify what he feels and means, and at the same time free to express and clarify what he himself means.[3]

But the fact is that this condition and this atmosphere are rare, and it is generally leaders who make it so. Suppose, in our hypothetical meeting, that we have a chairman who believes, even before the meeting, that new cushions must be secured at any price. After Jones issues his first blast involving the furnace the chairman is quite likely to do what he can at once to squelch Jones's type of objection. For instance he might say, "But I understand that we have only two more monthly payments, and we wouldn't have to start paying for the cushions until three months from now." The chairman would have his mind so firmly fixed on the task and on his own conviction about it that Jones, and whatever Jones meant, and whatever point Jones might have would be precisely what would receive no serious attention. Even should the cushions eventually be voted for, and even if Jones should feel compelled not to be nasty by voting nay, he would still feel unaccepted in the group. In all probability, this feeling of rejection would not stem from losing the battle, but from having his person *via* his convictions not taken seriously; that is, from having his negativities rejected in spirit as well as in content.

The chairman or leader of the group is crucial, especially at the beginning; for it is he who inevitably sets the tone and creates the atmosphere in which the group's operations proceed. If he ignores an expressed negative feeling, or argues against it in the light of his own convictions, or wholly agrees with it and says so, then a tone is set which other members are likely to follow. If he accepts Jones by accepting his right to have the feeling and manifests positive interest in what it means, he is setting a tone that will make for a freer and wider range of interaction in the group. This is not anarchy, but inclusion. It is not saying that anybody's ideas are as good as those of anyone else, but it does say that everyone has a right to have any ideas he has taken as seriously as discussion proves they deserve. The atmosphere is acceptance of the persons, including their right to ideas and feelings, positive or negative—but without an anarchistic drifting in which no one remembers that the group has a task to perform.

In connection with the meeting of any group, it is a wise rule of thumb to examine its operation equally from the point of view of *task* and from that of *process*. A productive group moves toward the performance of its task according to whatever timetable is set by circumstance. A genuinely interacting group accepts its members by paying attention to their ideas and feelings however negative in character. A group can be productive and yet not interactive; then it is authoritarian. It can be interactive but forget its task; in that case it is anarchic. There is now much evidence to suggest that, especially in small groups, it is the most genuinely interactive group that also becomes most productive.

Despite some excellent study that has been done in group dynamics, group therapy, and group leadership, and a good deal of experimentation along these lines in the churches, only recently has the first book applying the principles in church situations appeared. *The Group Workshop Way in the Church* by Paul F. Douglass is an introductory book, and many will find it helpful.[4] I could wish that the author might have dealt more directly and deeply with the function of negative feelings in group work.

The Group as Shepherd

Our brief discussion of group process has made it clear that here, as in one-to-one relationships, what is crucial is the way in which negative feelings are dealt with. To the extent that the persons are not accepted, to that extent will the group fail to become interactive. The acceptance of the persons and the conviction of its genuineness is tested finally by the acceptance of feelings and ideas that are experienced as negative. The group principle is the same as we have seen in the shepherding of individual persons.

There are, however, two types of obvious differences between the one-to-one and the group situations. The first is in the place and function of the leader or shepherd. In one-to-one relationships, his shepherding role and function remain constant—it is his function to accept, understand, and clarify. In a group relationship the leader may indeed have

148

to exercise most of the accepting and clarifying functions early in the group's operations. If at the tenth meeting, however, he is still performing all these functions with no assists from group members, the group has failed to become genuinely interactive. Thus it is especially helpful to think of the functions that need to be exercised to bring about real group interaction, but to associate these with their performance by and within the group and not solely in relation to the leader. So it is that an effective group leader rejoices when he perceives that more and more of the vital functions of accepting, understanding, and clarifying are being carried out by the group and its members. At the same time we know that a leader who attempts to force a group to perform these functions before they feel comfortable enough to try them is running the risk of anarchy. Group-centered leadership is the goal, but it is not a description of the process of the group's movement toward the goal.

The other obvious difference between the group and the one-to-one situations is the different conception of the task to be performed. When the one-to-one situations are dominantly shepherding in character, the task is helping the individual person to deal with his problem, in the performance of which much may have to be considered that was not at first felt to be relevant to that problem. In the vast majority of group situations, indeed in virtually all except those called "group therapy," the task is something in which various people have various kinds of stakes. In fact, unlike the one-to-one relationship, very seldom is a group situation so defined as to give any prominent place among its objectives to shepherding. This, we believe, is a mistake. Groups in the church, met for whatever specific purpose or task, are far more capable of performing shepherding functions at the same time than we have ever realized. The fact that these functions are likely to be performed indirectly rather than directly does not minimize the importance or the potentiality.

Let us return to our friend Jones, who opened the hypothetical meeting by indicating that the furnace bill was not yet paid. We suggested that, even if the money should be demonstrated as available, Jones might still be against new cushions, perhaps because his great-grandfather had given the old ones. Let us go on from here with some further hypotheses about Jones, assuming the truth of the great-grandfather idea. What *could* account for a current negative feeling in Jones just because his ancestor gave the old cushions? The answers could be various—perhaps the ancestor was rich, while Jones is poor and has a secret feeling he has come down in the world and brought his family's name with him; perhaps he is a miser, and his wife has been heckling him to give a memorial to the church as his ancestors did; perhaps his ancestor turned out to be a horse thief and Jones does not want the story raked up, and so on. Whatever should turn out to be the truth, some stake vital to Jones is involved symbolically in the pew cushion decision. This may be more or less clearly known to Jones, or to the other members of the committee. Whatever it is, Jones's self-respect is symbolically threatened. If the meeting, therefore, fails to accept Jones as a person by giving due attention to his ideas and feelings as expressed, it is also placing new pressures upon Jones's tottering self-respect. Neither the committee nor any member thereof may so intend; nevertheless, that will be the result. Jones will probably give up the battle in disgust, or make his defenses tighter than ever. In neither case will his self-respect be helped to find a firmer foundation in a fellowship that accepts even when it does not agree.

But suppose that Jones's expressed ideas and feelings are taken seriously, accepted although not necessarily agreed with. It is most unlikely that Jones, in this type of group with this kind of task, will say anything about self-respect, or horse thieves, or his wife's heckling. But if *he* is accepted, and his expressed ideas and feelings taken seriously, he will feel less need to rigidify his defenses. The result will be that he can experience and positively appreciate wider ranges of the group's interaction than would otherwise have been possible. He may be able to pay attention to Green's point of view in a genuine fashion, when before he would have listened only to strengthen his own arguments. The result can be a closer fellow feeling with Green. Even the expressed ideas that seem most alien and wrong to him may tweak him to ask himself what Smith really means, since he is obviously not stupid, and yet his idea at first seems so. As it slowly sinks in upon him that agreement is not the necessary precondition for respect, he may be able to express his own ideas and feelings more freely but with less emotion of the kind that promotes isolation. Result: Something positive has happened to his self-respect through the growing range of interaction within the group. A shepherding function has been performed for Jones over and above whatever the group has done to move toward accomplishing its task.

I am sure there is, and will be, an important place in the life of the church for cell groups, or prayer groups, or "class meetings," in which the dominant task is simply the enrichment—psychological or spiritual, or both—of the members. If such groups are proving useful in mental hospitals and theological schools, they can hardly be alien to the local church. Their function can be a kind of shepherding in unadulterated form.

Yet our history shows the greatest vitality in church groups when their task has transcended the enrichment of the members. Effective prayer meetings were for the praise of God and not solely the good of the members. The society with a missionary-aiding task might be more vital than the cell group. The young people's group with a project beyond itself might have more energy than that which discussed only immediate concerns.

What seems of the greatest importance is recognizing the shepherding potentialities inherent in all our smaller church groups. Precisely as in the case of Jones, the best shepherding by the fellowship may help Jones only indirectly with his personal need. Jones, at this time, is not prepared to face his problem as a problem head-on. If he were, he would go to his pastor and ask to discuss his problem of self-respect. Jones can come closer to admitting to himself that he has such a problem only as his defenses can be let down, and these can be let down only as he is accepted and his feelings and ideas taken seriously, even though they may not be agreed with. Thus, Jones is prepared only for shepherding help that comes indirectly. This is precisely what the proper kind of group operation can help him with. But note that this is just as genuinely shepherding as is the one-to-one relationship.

We are now in a position to return to the shrewd observation by John McNeill that it makes a difference whether two, or more than two, are gathered together. Where there are two, the personal problem is the task and is worked at directly. Where there are three or more, the shepherding is indirect and symbolic. In the first, the agreed on goal is, in some significant sense, the solution of the problem. In the second, the shepherding goal is to diminish the defenses through acceptance and understanding so that, if there is a problem, there will be readiness to seek help about it as may be appropriate to its nature.

According to this conception, then, the group may perform a shepherding function no less vital than that involved in one-to-one relationships, but of a different character. From this point of view we can and must value and cultivate genuine group interaction for its shepherding work, but not as a substitute for needed shepherding through one-to-one relationships. Indeed, it seems likely that the relationship between the two is reciprocal and mutually consequent rather than substitutionary. Good group work may help people to admit they have problems for which good individual work is necessary in terms of solution. Group shepherding may increase demand for individual shepherding. As a result of individual shepherding, persons may be capable of interaction in a group as never before; hence individual shepherding may increase both the quantity and quality of shepherding and sustenance through groups. Valuable as they are, group dynamics and group therapy can never be substitutes for work with individuals.

The Mutual Care of Souls

From the point of view that has been expressed here, what happens to McNeill's injunction to extend the uniquely Protestant emphasis on the mutual care or cure of souls? In speaking to this question, let us recall that shepherding is both more and less than has been meant in the tradition by the *cura animarum*. We have acknowledged the disciplinary aspects of the historic *cura* to be important and necessary to the fellowship, but we have contended that they belong under another rubric than shepherding. On the other hand, we have held that much that has gone under vague names like "edification" in the tradition is dominantly shepherding and have broadened that term beyond the attempt to meet obvious and openly acknowledged inner need.

From our point of view, then, the "care of souls" is shepherding when the dominant concern at this time is the souls being cared for. When necessity compels the subordination of the souls to the welfare of the fellowship, then shepherding, for the time being, becomes subsidiary. From the shepherding perspective consideration of the "mutual care of souls," therefore, has reference to the now dominant concern for the souls or, in our modern language, for the persons.

It would seem that there are three ways in which shepherding as the "mutual care of souls" should and can be advanced by Protestant Christians. The first is to rethink the meaning of pastor-parishioner relationships under this heading. The Protestant pastor holds no special keys to heaven. Neither he nor his calling are better in God's eyes than are other men and their callings. He is to be a Christian like any Christian, called of God into his calling as they into theirs. What is to distinguish him from other Christians is his competence including, among other things, his ability as a shepherd. So considered, competence is a function, not a state or condition. His best shepherding is fully "mutual" in that he is as likely to have the problems as the person he is trying to help. It is of course not mutual in the sense of irresponsible swapping of stories. The atmosphere is mutual; the content is the parishioner's need. Rethinking of this kind will help to restore the shepherding work of the pastor with individual persons to its proper place under the "mutual care of souls."

The second thing that can be done is to foster more shepherding of the indirect kind that has been described in the ongoing smaller groups of the church. It is not, heaven forbid, that we have more groups and new groups. The fact is that our churches are so full of groups with only a task-centered conception of their function that potential shepherding is simply regarded as irrelevant and even undesirable. This plainly rests upon a misunderstanding of group life and the Christian premises that lie behind it. Knowledge, patience, and thoughtful interpretation of the possibilities can all do much to help our many church groups become more interactive (and therefore, to perform indirectly more shepherding functions) while actually, in the long run, increasing their productivity in relation to their tasks. This too is an expansion of the "mutual care of souls." For initial interpretation one can translate this phrase into the "mutual paying attention to what the other fellow is really trying to say, no matter how silly or stupid it sounds."

There is a third way to advance the "mutual care of souls," not mentioned hitherto, which involves what may be called the "helping expertness of the laity." A great many discussions of the place and function of laymen and women in the church proceed as if they were all alike—as if the one important thing about them were that they do not know as much as the minister about what matters. But in our own day at least, the fact is that there is a growing number of dedicated Christian laymen and women who are far more

155

competent than the minister about many aspects of the church's task, including some aspects of shepherding. It is the height of irresponsibility to speak of psychiatrists and other physicians, of clinical psychologists, of social workers, and of others in related professions, as if they were "secular" and only the minister were "sacred" or "Christian." To be sure, there are still many in these rapidly growing helping professions who make no Christian profession, but the proportion seems less year by year. Certainly there is a great number of such people, as fully Christian as any minister, and in some aspects of the shepherding of persons more competent than any minister. Technically they are laymen, but on some aspects of shepherding they are experts.

It is high time we recognized in appropriate ways that these professional helpers who are also Christians are engaged, every hour of their working lives, in implementing the Christian ideal of the "mutual care of souls." Are we Americans so parochial minded that we cannot perceive these persons as performing the "mutual care of souls" on behalf of the church unless they are holding their interviews in a church building, receiving their compensation from the church treasurer, and substituting a Bible or prayer book for the tools proper to their profession?

There may indeed be occasions and people and churches when some such Christian layman as a psychiatrist or social worker may be put on the payroll of a local church or a council of churches, in order to aid with aspects of the ministry of shepherding at which he is expert. But for every such person, there are dozens, even hundreds, who do their best to administer their helping work under the aegis of their professions instead of becoming, administratively, a

156

part of the visible church structure. What is vital is that they be helped to exercise their Christian priesthood in the very acts of performing their professional helping functions, and that the whole fellowship recognize what they are doing as part of the "mutual care of souls." The minister is not the sole shepherd of the church, but neither are all laymen to be lumped together as if the shepherding skill of one were the same as that of every other.

Finally, there are of course other laymen with no claim to any form of professional expertness in relation to shepherding. But unprofessional does not mean incompetent or unskilled. Some wise women of middle age, whose spirits have expanded and not contracted during the vicissitudes of feeding husbands and rearing children, may have capacities for shepherding selected persons in need—some older people, for example—as well as or better than could the pastor or other professional helpers. In those situations in which the primary needs are friendly concern, wise sharing of wisdom, and breaking the barriers of isolation, there are far more resources in every local church than we have yet learned how to harness. To be sure, with any human relations on behalf of the church fellowship, progress should be slow and careful. There are more resources here, demanding more in terms of organizational skill by the minister than in previous centuries, than we have dreamed of.

Conclusion

We have nowhere asserted that shepherding is *the* function of the fellowship, as if the mind of the church were to be on nothing but the special needs of individual persons and not also on the worship of God, the communication of the Christian message, and the making of a coherent member of Christ's body out of each unit of the fellowship. But we have asserted that shepherding is a constant, inescapable, and valuable function of the fellowship—and that through the concretizing of the generic fellowship in the particular fellowship at least an indirect shepherding function of high desirability is being performed. This is not, we have contended, a substitute for the individual shepherding of persons by the pastor, or by other Christian professional helpers. But in terms of the full meaning of shepherding, we have held it to be no less important.

X. THE SEVEN AGES OF SHEPHERDING

Since the object of the verb shepherding is the person or persons, it is plain that no shepherding generalizations must be permitted to obscure the range and variety that is inherent in concrete human individuality. In his recent, excellent book *Becoming* Gordon W. Allport wisely warns us against any psychology so preoccupied with universal principles that it loses sight of concrete individuality, which is most outstanding in human beings as "manifest uniqueness of organization." [1] Yet Allport proceeds, wisely and without inconsistency, to set forth certain general principles that will enable us better to understand personality, including its individuality and uniqueness.

It is our intention in the following discussion to follow a somewhat similar course. Not only do we not want to obscure individualities, we want to lift them up as sharply as possible. The road to this kind of understanding is through interaction of the individuality with general principles. Such general principles, as relevant to shepherding, may be of several kinds. They may be relational, as we have already discussed in Chapter 2. They could be about different cultures and classes, as indicated in chapter 5, about differences between the sexes, or about other relevant things. We have elected to concentrate on those principles that follow from an understanding of man as a chronological pilgrim—man's development from infancy to old age.

Two questions will be in our minds throughout this discussion. First: What, generally and statistically speaking, are the desirabilities and potentialities of human development at this or that particular stage or period? Second: What specifically do these general truths contribute to the shepherding function in relation to specific people at these stages or periods?

We shall address ourselves first to a quick review of the basic needs, tasks, characteristics, problems, and potentialities that seem to inhere in each of the seven ages of man's pilgrimage. We shall then discuss the implications for Christian shepherding that emerge from this developmental account.

Developmental Stages

The seven ages we shall distinguish, not wholly arbitrarily, are as follows, infancy, up to about two years; childhood, from infancy to preadolescence; preadolecence, the two or three years preceding puberty; adolescence, from puberty to the early twenties; young adulthood, from the early twenties until thirty-five or forty; middle adulthood, from thirty-five or forty to sixty or sixty-five; and older adulthood, beyond sixty or sixty-five.

Infancy. The little baby's capacity for relatedness to others is dependent upon his fundamental needs' being satisfied by the persons in his environment. He must have food, warmth, safety, cuddling, and gurgles. If not supplied by other persons, he has no way of meeting these needs for himself. If the needs are met, the baby will be outgoing in the sense of being related positively to environing persons, although by no means necessarily extraverted. As he moves on through the later stages of infancy, the relative security he feels as a result of being able to trust environing persons to meet his needs will enable him to begin to distinguish his own individuality, or his selfhood. Through play he exercises his capacity both for relatedness and for individuality. His world of experience includes things. And what he learns from contact with things—textures, touches, temperatures, colors—also helps him in dealing with the world of people, including himself. In some respects his service to the world seems entirely subordinated to concern for his own fulfillment. But since the world seems to love him, and not regard him as morally reprehensible for his concentration on intake at the expense of output, he is probably right in concluding, "They also serve who only coo and gurgle."

Childhood. Between the ages of two and ten or eleven, the child is almost as dependent, in basic respects, upon his parents as he was when an infant. Nevertheless, the striking fact of his social relatedness is the growing importance to him of his peers. Quite normally, he has ups and downs in the capacity for and interest in his relations with other people. Language enters during this period, and its major function becomes the providing of a most subtle and discriminating basis of communication in his relationships. With the normal ups and downs, his individuality increases during this period, and so do his skills. Play, study, and hobbies become, for him, sometimes merged and sometimes sharply and arbitrarily segregated. His acquaintance with the world of things is greatly aided by the fact of language, and affects his relationship with the world of persons. His own fulfillment is adjusted prudentially (part of the time) to the interests of others, even on rare occasions to the desires of his parents. He learns that he can please or not please as he chooses, if he will take the consequences either way. But he has not yet interiorized a genuine love feeling for other people. His service is still prudence, not a part of

161

what is essential for his own fulfillment. His intellectual development is prodigious during these years in its scope and range, but does not yet include the ability to grasp abstractions and know that they are abstractions.

Preadolescence. Of all the periods up to middle adulthood, the preadolescent is that about which our understanding is most inadequate. Yet it is not, as even Freud apparently thought, a mere combination of the rounding off of childhood and the taking of a deep breath before puberty. It has autonomously significant tasks, problems, and needs of its own. Of first importance seems the wholly new kind of interior capacity for relatedness. For the first time the person is able, indeed is inwardly compelled, to regard and feel the interests of another as being as important to him as are his own interests. This new capacity is internal and not directly visible, unlike the approaching changes of puberty. It may, therefore, feel all the more dangerous. Until it has been lived with and managed, its exercise must be carefully guarded or one will be invaded. So the relational discriminations are at first narrow and often arbitrary. Last week Pete was a great fellow; now he's nuts. The last persons to be beneficiaries of the new capacities are, properly enough, parents. In terms of mental development, the preadolescent seems to begin dimly to see abstractions as abstractions; and thus, in the world of the mind as in that of relationship, to take his first and most important stride from childhood to adulthood. For the first time the future begins to become significant to him and he can grasp it as a general concept. In a limited, and what seems to adults an arbitrary, way he is capable of seeing service as an essential aspect of fulfillment.

Adolescence. The most obvious facts about adolescent development are the suddenly emerging interest in the other sex and the movement through education toward job. Puberty is the beginning of the maturation of adult sexual capacity; and adolescence is the period in which, as Harry Stack Sullivan put it, one attempts to learn how to bring "lust" and "intimacy" together.[2] Occupational preparation becomes increasingly serious. Rational thought, work, and planning increase, with backslidings into bobby sox, panty raids, Elvis Presley, and sometimes more harmful forms of hoodlumism. If a hobby be defined as a seriously pursued interest not for profit, then adolescence witnesses a sharper separation of hobby from work than ever before. For a fortunate minority education and consequent job may mean in part a fulfillment in themselves. For many they may be regarded only as the least uncomfortable means toward ends that lie elsewhere. For the first time there are consciously considered problems of the relation of fulfillment and service. If prematurely identified (so-called adolescent "idealism"), they may result in either social blindness or eventual disillusionment and cynicism. If completely separated, there is a threat to the place and function of each in the person's life. As never before, there is the possibility of either inflation or deflation of a basic self-respect.

Young Adulthood. On the basis of a statistical definition of normality, the most important relational fact of young adulthood is marriage. Especially under the "romantic" pattern of marriage, now growing quantitatively in our society, marriage is expected to center and contain nearly all of life's relationships. With the family as a husband-wife-children affair only, very great demands are placed upon the marriage relationship to fulfill many kinds of personal needs. Both husband and wife are very busy; she with house, children, and often job besides; he with getting ahead in his job, doing it himself with his house, and being pals with his children at night and on week ends. Perhaps, as he sees his baby carefully explore a texture or a color, he has a twinge of remembrance that he too once explored things for their own sake; but now, for the most part, things to him are simply means to the end of his family's fulfillment. He is unaware of having become an antisacramentalist. Within the bounds of his family he makes an almost complete equation of fulfillment and service. But too often he and his wife seem so busy that service extends only a short distance beyond the kitchen door. The family's first beyond-the-yard experiments with service are likely to be prudential, Sunday school for the children before church for parents, local playground committee before city planning, and the like. For it must be recalled by those beyond the age of changing diapers, that this is a busy, active, heavily scheduled, and emotionally outgoing period of life. It is not, for most, a period providing either the time or the stimulus to reflection, but there are very many exceptions.

Middle Adulthood. With the possible exception of pre-adolescence, the middle ages are the least understood of the whole pilgrimage. One of the reasons for this is that most of the people who try to examine the pilgrimage reflectively are in this group, and it is always easier to be honest about the other fellow than about ourselves. The obvious general fact of this period is the need to shift life's values from the dimension of breadth and extensiveness to that of depth and intensive cultivation. By this time, either there are two cars in the garage or there probably never will be. Either way the attitude toward cars must become different from what it was at twenty-five, when the second-hand jalopy would do for awhile. By this age either the children are born and pretty well along in school, or there are not likely to be any. Either the mode of making relationships is established with some satisfaction, or it is likely to remain confused for the rest of life. It is at this period that we find the peak incidence figures for divorce among couples whose marriage has lasted at least a year, the peak for adultery among educated persons, the peak incidence of alcohol and drug addiction, and the peak for a great many other kinds of socially conditioned personality ills. One important factor in the incidence of all of these is the extreme difficulty of making the inner perspective transition from the "more and more" point of view of young adulthood, which can always feel it possible, if necessary, to change jobs or even wives, to that of middle adulthood, which cannot do so with impunity. "Successful" people in middle years often find the "more and more" inwardly palling, but cannot admit it to themselves, because these are the values on which their lives have been built. "Unsuccessful" people find it equally difficult to admit that they are now never likely to achieve the values they have set. At a time when the relation to things—the ability to indulge again in a serious hobby for no other reason than its enjoyment—becomes possible, things may be regarded as incapable of bearing anything but a "more and more" means relationship to one's fulfillment. In a way not possible in the frenzied activity of young adulthood, the relationship of service to fulfillment may now be changed and brought into closer connection. If the separation has become too ingrained, however, this will not take place, and one will go on taking and getting only, because "if you don't look after yourself, nobody else will." For a great many married

165

couples relationships become dull for reasons that have nothing to do with budgets, sexual capacity, or in-laws. The romantic excitement, including early child rearing, is gone; and nothing solid has been built to replace it. Men are inclined to take love for granted, but to seek excitement in various forms and degrees, all the way from stenographic adultery, to counting the panties on the clothesline next door. Women are not above extreme forms of the same indulgences, but seem more likely to seek evidences of approbation and reassurance that they are still attractive through social relationships—for example, by being able to hold a strange and handsome man in rapt conversation for a ten-minute stretch at a party. With all this, it must be repeated that this period is so close to the examiner that much of it misses the eye. Unlike all previous periods, as Carl Jung has rightly noted, the revolution in perspective that is required in the middle years does not come automatically. It requires initiative and co-operation and often a painful confrontation of new reality on our part. If that initiative is not taken, the consequences may be severe, but slow and apparently due to something else.

Older Adulthood. When I worked with Paul B. Maves and J. Lennart Cedarleaf some years ago on the first comprehensive study of *Older People and the Church,* we found ourselves coming again and again, by different routes, to the conclusion that older people are what they were before only more so.[3] Many of the characteristics wrongly attributed to the older years themselves are not so caused, but are merely the result of bringing into the open factors previously kept down by circumstance. A woman who in middle years took care of six children, various dogs and cats, and a lazy husband, and always looked harried, now reveals in later years great positive capacities for human relatedness and sensitive appreciation of aesthetic realities. Another woman, who had always bustled about with a great many things to do with her husband and children, now sits disconsolately and blames her plight on old age, when the fact is she never learned the capacity to take initiative and to engage in any activity for its own sake. Both persons are now what they always were only more so. Certainly the older years usually mean that the quantity of relatedness must be more limited. This, however, makes it possible for the quality to become deeper. Relationships may, for the first time, become deeper yet less intense—always excepting the walrus-mustached gentlemen escorting chorus girls on their arms. One's selfhood now obviously cannot be a matter of "more and more," or of onward and upward. Either one learns to live with himself during the middle years, or he finds it uncommonly difficult in older years. As to things, there must be more selectivity. Considering the serious economic plight of a great mass of older people in our society, this may be putting the cart before the horse. Nevertheless, things again have the potentiality of a sacramental relationship. Their service may seem again more than a means to an end—a relationship to be respected in an I-Thou kind of sense. The actualities of service may be limited, but such service as one can render will be more likely to be viewed as an aspect of fulfillment. Above all we need to note that all other ages in our society except the very young look ambiguously at the older years. Older people remind the rest of us of contraction, of decline, of limits, and of death. Rather than come to terms with these impending realities as our own problems, we are quite likely to feel negatively toward older people in secret, while revering such things as golden weddings publicly. This makes an extra problem for older people, but it is one that must be solved by others before reaching the golden years themselves.

Shepherding the Ages

The first contribution to our shepherding of persons that can be made by an understanding of developmental stages is to free us from preoccupation with some obvious but secondary details and to help us to concentrate on some fundamentals that are less obtrusive. When we stand aside and take a long look at the several stages in the human pilgrimage some unexpected similarities and contrasts appear.

For example, in certain very basic senses, the period of childhood is like that of young adulthood. The child from two to ten, and the adult from legal maturity to the forties, both have pretty well laid out for them the tasks to be performed. Quite properly, both see life in terms of expansion, of learning or of doing more. Life is a business of onward and upward. The mood of both periods is extraverted.

In certain very striking respects, we find basic commonalities between adolescence and older adulthood. In both these periods, inner change is absolutely forced or compelled by circumstance which is outer, in that the person cannot control it. The adolescent cannot prevent his physical growth and sexual maturation. They come whether he wants them or not, and they are obvious. They compel an inner alteration in his views, values, and feelings. Similarly, the older adult, whether he likes it or not, finds his physical strength declining, which in turn affects the kind and quantity of work and other activities in which he can engage. This too is obvious, and provokes a change in his feelings and attitudes within. In these very basic respects, older adults and teen-

168

agers are alike, and it may not be without significance that these are the two groups about which society in general feels most ambiguous.

But perhaps the most profound similarity of all is that between the preadolescent and the adult of middle years. Childhood and young adulthood, as we saw, are periods of extraverted mood; adolescence and older adulthood are ages of forced revolution. Preadolescence and middle adulthood are properly periods of introverted mood. They are periods in which *internal* revolution should take place by internal initiative. But because the results are not obvious, and the needed change is not compelled by outer circumstance, it may be avoided or ignored. The basic task of the preadolescent is accepting and coming to terms with his new inner capacity to feel the interests of the other as being as important to him as are his own interests. The basic task of middle adulthood is the shift from an expansionist, onward and upward, bigger and better, externally oriented kind of psychology to an attitude of contraction but with new depth, to a new reflectiveness and selectivity, to a new scale of values determined by one's choice rather than by outer circumstance.

It is my conviction that a long look of this kind at the basic tasks, functions, and needs of each stage in life's pilgrimage can be of genuine help in our shepherding of persons both by sensitizing us to meanings that might otherwise elude us, and by correcting wrong meanings that we might otherwise read in.

For instance, suppose we are asked to help a man of middle years who says there is trouble between him and his wife. When he gives details, they sound pallid—uncapped tooth paste tubes, burned toast, the car not put in the garage. The fact is not of course that marital troubles are caused by little rather than by big things. The fact is rather that in early married years, the hustle and bustle of romance, of job, and of children kept this couple in tolerable accommodation with each other; but now that job is secure it is dull, wife is routine and she is dull too, and children are beginning to leave home and one feels a bit more useless. This man suffers from a meaninglessness which previous circumstance prevented him from feeling. To the extent that this is true (and it may have a million variations in any particular person), we confront quite a different shepherding task from that of the following situation.

Here a man in his late twenties consults us about ostensibly the same problem, trouble between himself and his wife. He begins with unwashed dishes but quickly works up to bigger things. With some justice and evidence he suspects his wife of seeing another man occasionally, as well as of neglecting her children and him. He finally confesses that some of the evenings he was supposed to have been working were spent in noninnocent fashion, although he says he is sorry and would like to make the marriage work. This is certainly different from the previous situation we have described. Here too is a form of meaninglessness, but of a more rebellious kind than that in our adult of middle years. It is more immediately troublesome; the possible consequences of broken marriage would be more obviously serious for more people. On the other hand, if the shepherding of this situation now is more than a mere palliation of symptoms, basic meaning can be brought into the lives of this couple so that when they reach middle years they will not confront the tepid and boring disillusionment experienced by the man we have already mentioned. The danger is greater, but the rewards of effective shepherding may also be much greater. How foolish it would be to treat both situations solely as if they were to be seen as husband-wife conflicts, without appreciation of these subtle but very significant differences.

No human being at any age, even the tiniest baby, is to be understood solely on the basis of his stage in life's pilgrimage, as if all the varieties of his individuality, which increase rather than decrease with the years, were unimportant. Yet how important it may be to correct our own vision of what something means to a person by a better understanding of the basic needs, tasks, and problems of his stage in the course of life. Suppose, for instance, that our man in middle-adult years had come to a pastor who was himself a young adult. Being in the period of an extraverted mood, the young pastor is likely to explore tirelessly for some specific cause of the difficulty, and to feel more and more baffled as he learns that the man's job is secure and more or less satisfying, that the sex life of the couple is fine, and that the children are not delinquents. With no awareness of what he is doing, he may be reading his own young adult patterns into the situation and thus be failing genuinely to accept or to understand the situation of the man he is trying to help.

Conversely, suppose our young man in the twenties consults a pastor of middle years. The pastor has been through this period of turbulence. Perhaps his wife had her faults in taking care of him and rearing their children. No doubt he, if honest, will admit to himself that a sweater or an ankle has occasionally caught his attention. He may feel he conquered all temptation, and all that is needed in such situations is something he may call "strength of character."

171

If he does think and feel this way, he too will project something irrelevant into the young man he is trying to help, and will fail to perform the basic functions of accepting and understanding. So each man, if he takes seriously the stages of life, can find something that will help to correct his own vision, and thus enable him to be a shepherd to greater varieties and conditions of men.

There are some obvious and some unobvious but important things about the shepherding of persons at various ages. Infants and children are of course to be shepherded mainly through their parents. But in the church program for children—Sunday, week day, or camp—do we not sometimes forget that there may be vital shepherding functions to be performed as well as the communication of the gospel? Lumping this together as "religious education" runs the danger of obscuring the need for and the means of shepherding. When my colleague Granger Westberg was in a local church, he sent cards to the children aged eight or nine in his parish inviting them for an appointment to talk with him. At first they were scared, but when they saw he wanted to become acquainted, they relaxed and were very proud of having an "interview" with the pastor. As a foundation for needed shepherding, such direct contacts deserve more attention than they have received.

Ordinarily the pre-adolescent has not reached a very verbal stage, and our shepherding of him must be mainly through parents and through groups. But the cautious opportunity to enable him to put a little of his new inward capacity for relatedness on an admired church-school teacher, scoutmaster, or pastor is to be encouraged. If things get bad, he may prove to have an astonishing capacity to verbalize about what is taking place.

172

Adolescents are our pride and our despair. They can talk but, for the most part, they won't. Perhaps we shall have to breed a whole new group of pastoral specialists with youth, but I hope and believe not—apart from some specialists of talent who can point the way to others. He who would shepherd teen-agers must get rid of sentimental or ambiguous feelings about them, and walk the delicate line in which he accepts and understands them on the one side, but does not necessarily support their views and practices against their parents and the adult world on the other.

As to the shepherding of adults, we have already noted and illustrated some of the obvious and unobvious requirements. There is no reason why a pastor of any age cannot prove an effective shepherd to persons of quite different ages, provided he is alert to the individuality that is present and uses his knowledge of developmental stages to prevent projecting his own feelings irrelevantly into the other. Indeed, there may be special danger in his shepherding of persons in his own age bracket. He may wrongly assume that what is normal in his feelings is normal in theirs, which may well be false. In any event, knowledge of the stages can be of great benefit to shepherding.

The Hero and the Prodigal

There is a basic similarity and a basic difference between the way in which Christian faith, and the best insights of sages in all lands and eras, have viewed the meaning of the human pilgrimage. In the interesting book by Joseph Campbell *The Hero with a Thousand Faces* we have a remarkable picture of how, through the myths of the hero, human wisdom has interpreted this pilgrimage.[4]

The pattern of all the hero myths is threefold—separation, trial, and return. As the myth opens, the hero is summoned to leave. The herald who summons him is both familiar and mysterious; he points to a mysterious land that is to be visited, and hints at the hazards of reaching it. At first the hero refuses; he would prefer to stay home; eventually he decides to go.

He then enters upon the trials and hazards, which may be dark forests or raging seas. He undergoes various trials, one of which is climactic. He feels some hitherto unknown power helping him especially with the climactic trial—such as the battle with the dragon. Although he is nearly spent, he hangs on, receives new support from the mysterious power, and conquers the dragon. With the dragon dead, the scene is desolate and horrible, but it is not all desolation. A princess appears; if she is sleeping, she soon wakens; if she is ugly, she becomes beautiful. The hero and the princess plight their troth, and are often then waited on by a father figure, a universal father, who is plainly not the same as the father of the village back home.

Then comes the return. The hero, complete with princess, enters the village back home. The men there have not done what he has done, and he has to endure being different. His isolation is mitigated in some way, usually by his becoming the ruler or father of the village. Still, although he has fought and won, and is held on a pedestal as a hero, he experiences an isolation he had not known in the early days. And while he loves his princess, she is, after all, only a woman.

Let us contrast this with the Christian myth interpreting the same events through the same pattern of separation, trial, and return, namely, the story of the Prodigal Son.[5] The son's motive for leaving his father's house is ambiguous, but the far country is mysteriously attractive. The son seems unaware of any conflict about leaving. Unlike the village father of the hero, this father is the universal father from the beginning. He respects his son's freedom and gives him his share of the inheritance. The son believes everything is onward and upward.

But when the far country is reached, the son sports himself for a time and then discovers that the pleasures are not what he had thought. He becomes vulnerable and fails. Indeed, some power not himself seems to drag him down. Whatever dragons there be are not slain. His forest is irremediably dark, and since it is a pig pen, possesses not even the stark dignity of the trees. There is no victory here, actually nor possibly. There is only failure, which must be acknowledged. The one hope lies in return to request mercy and forgiveness.

The return is not made by a conquering hero with gift-wrapped dragon-hide boxes to distribute in the old home town. It is made in humility, and without expectation beyond the mild hope for forgiveness. This is a radically different son from him who went forth to the far country. The father, however, has not changed. Only now, due to the change in attitude of his son, can the father show the depth and universality of his love. Forgiveness is not a cautious, legally regulated tidbit, but a feast of full and complete acceptance. To show the superiority of the Prodigal Son's humility, the grumbling older brother enters the picture— unable alike to accept his father's love or to feel the need for it, except in envy.

The similarities in the two stories should not be set aside too quickly. Both view life realistically. There are trials to be encountered, and dangers to be met. Man cannot remain at a former stage without moving, like the Prodigal Son's older brother. He must move out through the trials, and eventually return home.

But the differences are enormous. The hero leaves home because he must; the Prodigal, because he is given freedom by his father. The hero conquers his trials, and feels a mysterious power supporting him; the Prodigal loses every trial, and his mysterious power helps to drag him down. The hero gains a princess; the Prodigal winds up with the pigs. The hero is commended by a new father who, however, does not promise to take anything from his shoulders; the Prodigal returns to the same father who, however, reveals his love precisely when it is most needed. The hero is feted, but with the result of feeling different, apart, and isolated; the Prodigal is welcomed with rejoicing and love unlimited.

Granted that there is depth of insight into the meaning of the human pilgrimage in both these myths, Christians feel there is something much more basic in the second than in the first. The Prodigal leaves, not because he must, but because he is free. He leaves in order to seek his fulfillment, not cluttered up with dragon-slaying equipment. Succeed or fail in his immediate aims, life fails him, and no mysterious power of positive thinking assures him that what he wanted all along was fine, so just keep at it. He fails ignominiously, but the acknowledgment of his failure, instead of being merely negative, sets his feet upon the path back home. No conquering hero he, but one who hardly dares hope, at the most, even for mercy. And mercy, forgiveness, and love are there in unconditional measure. Now he sees the father who was like this all along but whom his eyes had not perceived.

The hero is ambiguous about his *separation* and his *re-*

turn. While engaged in his trials, he is unambiguous and unconquerable. The Prodigal is unambiguous about his *separation;* he wants to go and that is all there is to it. He is met unambiguously on his return. He is completely loved and accepted, and that is all there is to that. His trial has hardly even the dignity of ambiguity, so complete a failure is it. But it *is* ambiguous, since the freedom exercised is good, while the way it is exercised brings failure.

Every man must be separated, leave home, exercise his freedom and make mistakes that bring him to his knees in failure more than once. The trials of each stage are different but equally real and equally crucial. During each stage there must be a return home, and a humble acceptance of the love and forgiveness that have been always there, but which we have not been able to perceive. It is the shepherding function of the church to help persons at every age to look with equal honesty at the failure of their trials and their values, and at the new dimensions now revealed in the love of God through Jesus Christ.

REFERENCES

CHAPTER I *The Gospel and Shepherding*

1. Luke 15:3-7; Matt. 18:12-13.
2. The reader interested in an elaboration of these distinctions may consult my *Preface to Pastoral Theology* (Nashville: Abingdon Press, 1958).
3. *Ibid.*
4. Heb. 13:20 R.S.V.
5. Rom. 8:17.
6. I Cor. 12:12 ff.; Rom. 12:4 ff.
7. See John 10 and 21.
8. Luke 8:26 ff.
9. See, for example, the forthcoming book on the unitary conception of mental illness by Karl Menninger and colleagues, to be published by Harcourt, Brace, and Company.
10. I have elaborated this point in Chapter 6 of *Preface to Pastoral Theology*.
11. See Menninger, *op. cit.*

CHAPTER II *Basic Principles of Shepherding*

1. Among the best discriminating evaluations are Paul E. Johnson, *Psychology of Pastoral Care* (Nashville: Abingdon Press, 1953); Wayne E. Oates, *The Christian Pastor* (Philadelphia: The Westminster Press, 1951); and Carroll A. Wise, *Pastoral Counseling: Its Theory and Practice* (New York: Harper and Bros., 1951).
2. Paul Tillich, *The Courage to Be* (New Haven, Conn.: Yale University Press, 1952).
3. See Freud, *A General Introduction to Psychoanalysis* (New York: Liveright Publishing Corporation, 1935), pp. 259 ff.
4. See my *The Counselor in Counseling* (Nashville: Abingdon Press, 1952).

CHAPTER III *Shepherding Grief and Loss*

1. The first publication was Erich Lindemann, "Symptomatology and Management of Acute Grief," *American Journal of Psychiatry*, 1944. See also Paul E. Irion, *The Funeral and the Mourners* (Nashville: Abingdon Press, 1954); Edgar N. Jackson, *Understanding Grief* (Nashville: Abingdon Press, 1957); and William F. Rogers, *Ye Shall Be Comforted* (Philadelphia: The Westminster Press, 1950).
2. Erich Lindemann, in oral communication.

CHAPTER IV *Shepherding the Family*

1. See George H. Mead, *Mind, Self and Society* (Chicago: The University of Chicago Press, 1934); and Paul E. Pfuetze, *The Social Self* (New York: Bookman Associates, 1954).
2. For instance, see R. A. Spitz's articles in *The Psychoanalytic Study of the Child* (New York: International Universities Press, 1945 and 1946), Volumes I and II.
3. For a "theology of parent-child relationships," see Reuel L. Howe, *Man's Need and God's Action* (Greenwich, Conn.: The Seabury Press, 1953). For an excellent recent analysis of the contemporary family situation from the Christian point of view, see Gibson Winter, *Love and Conflict: New Patterns in Family Life* (New York: Doubleday and Company, 1958).
4. Martha Wolfenstein, "Fun Morality: An Analysis of Recent American Child-Training Literature," *Childhood in Contemporary Cultures*, edited by Margaret Mead and Martha Wolfenstein (Chicago: The University of Chicago Press, 1955). Used by permission.
5. (New York: W. W. Norton and Company, 1928), pp. 84-85. Used by permission.
6. Some case reports of this kind are given in Part IV of *Marriage Consulting: An Introduction to Marriage Counseling*, by Rex A. Skidmore, Hulda Van Streeter Garrett, and C. Jay Skidmore (New York: Harper and Brothers, 1956), although the point of view is not the same as mine.

CHAPTER V *Shepherding and the Class Structure*

1. Perhaps the best book for the beginner in this area is W. Lloyd Warner, *Democracy in Jonesville* (New York: Harper and Brothers, 1949).
2. *Ibid.*, Chapter 6.
3. For a summary see Chapter 4, "Sex Patterns and Culture," in my *Sex Ethics and the Kinsey Reports* (New York: Association Press, 1953).
4. John Dollard presents a summary in Chapter 8, "Drinking Mores of the Social Classes," in *Alcohol, Science and Society* (New Haven, Conn.: Quarterly Journal of Studies on Alcohol, 1945).

CHAPTER VI *Shepherding Organization Men*

1. *The Organization Man* (New York: Simon and Schuster, 1956).
2. *The Lonely Crowd* (New Haven, Conn.: Yale University Press, 1950).
3. *Man for Himself* (New York: Rinehart and Company, 1947).
4. *Modern Man in Search of a Soul* (New York: Harcourt, Brace, and Company, 1933).
5. *Art and Artist* (New York: Alfred A. Knopf, 1932).
6. *The Protestant Era* (Chicago: The University of Chicago Press, 1948), Chapters III and IV.
7. Whyte, *op. cit.*, p. 420.
8. *Ibid.*, p. 282.

CHAPTER VII *Shepherding Rebels*

1. *Changing Values in College* (New York: Harper and Bros., 1957), pp. 3-4. Used by permission.

CHAPTER VIII *Shepherding Housewives*

1. See Jung, *op. cit.*, Chapter V on ''The Stages of Life.''

CHAPTER IX *Shepherding through Fellowship*

1. (New York: Harper and Bros., 1951), pp. 327-328.
2. (Philadelphia: Muhlenberg Press, 1956), Chapter VII.
3. See Thomas Gordon, *Group-Centered Leadership* (Boston: Houghton Mifflin Company, 1955).
4. (New York: Association Press, 1956).

CHAPTER X *The Seven Ages of Shepherding*

1. (New Haven, Conn.: Yale University Press, 1955), p. 21.
2. *The Interpersonal Theory of Psychiatry* (New York: W. W. Norton and Company, 1953).
3. (Nashville: Abingdon Press, 1949).
4. (New York: Pantheon Books, 1949).
5. *Luke* 15:11-32.

INDEX

Acceptance: and agreement in shepherding, 30; and the class structure, 79 ff.; in groups, 150-51; more complex forms of, 32 ff.; relation to justification by faith, 30; relation to understanding, 34; in shepherding, 28 ff.; theological and psychological understanding of, 31; of the unacceptable in shepherding, 30
Adolescence, 162-63; shepherding in, 173; similarity to older adulthood, 168-69
Adults, shepherding of, 173
Agape, relation to concern, 34
Agreement, and acceptance in shepherding, 30
Allport, Gordon W., 159
Ambiguity: of family, 60; in family, 63-64
Anxiety: in child rearing, 58; and clarification, 37
Attitudes, within family, 60 ff.

Basic Principles of Shepherding, 24 ff.
Bereavement. *See* Grief
Bible, healing in, 21 ff.; *see also* Scripture
Biblical theology, 11
Body of Christ, 20
Brunner, Emil, 114

Campbell, Joseph, 173
Cases, as leading to principles, 25
Cases presented: Mr. Abel, 122; Pastor Barton (Mrs. Henshaw), 42-54; Bill and Sue, 70-74; Bob, 123-24; Brilliant Woman, 33-34; Mrs. Fry (Pastor Kell), 25-38; Mrs. Henshaw (Pastor Barton), 42-54; Pastor Kell (Mrs. Fry), 25-38; Pew-Cushion Committee, 143-47; Priscilla Sellers, 80-84; Mrs. Supervisor, 89-90; Pastor Zarvis (Mrs. Zendt), 105-10; Mrs. Zendt (Pastor Zarvis), 105-10
Cedarleaf, J. Lennart, 166
Cell groups, 151
Changing attitudes, in family, 60 ff.
Chicago, The University of, 127
Childhood, 161-62; shepherding in, 172; similarity to young adulthood, 168
Christian ethics, 11
Christian family, 65 ff.

Faith, and culture, 11

Family: ambiguity in, 60; Christian, 65 ff.; and church, 68; as educational unit, 66; as established by God, 66; forms of problems in, 58; the "good," 67; grace in, 67; the ideal of, 68; monogamy in, 66; need for judgment in, 67-68; need for regeneration in, 67; need for shepherding, 65 ff.; as prime factor in self-formation, 57; relation of sexes in, 66; as serving both personal and social needs, 66; the shepherding of, 57 ff.; and the sovereignty of God, 67-68; the universal priesthood in, 66-67; voluntary commitment in, 68

Feelings: clarification of positive and negative, 36; concrete nature of, 36; of inferiority, 39; negative, acceptance of, 29-30; negative, differences in content of, 57; negative, guilt over, 38; negative, reappearance of, 32 ff.; negative, in shepherding, 29 ff.; relation of positive to negative, 35

Fellowship, and shepherding, 141 ff.

Femininity: and the class structure, 94-95; and inwardness, 137

Freud, Sigmund, 31, 36, 37, 102

Fromm, Erich, 97

Fulfillment and service, 88 ff.; Christian view of relation between, 92-93

Functions necessary for group operation, 149

Fun-morality, 65

Future life, and grief, 54

Gadarene, 21-22

Garrett, Hulda Van S., 180

Gordon, Thomas, 181

Gospel: and specific need, 17; basis of shepherding, 14 ff.

Grace, in family, 67

Great commission, 18

Grief: comfort in and through, 51; cultural pressures about, 53; emptiness in, 51; fear of emotion in, 50; and future life, 54; process of, 51; the shepherding of, 42 ff.; special responsibilities of pastor in shepherding of, 42; spiritual strength in, 50; work of, 51

Group: anarchic, 148; authoritarian, 148; interactive, 147; productive, 147; as shepherd, 148 ff.; shepherding through, 141 ff.; shepherding is indirect, 152-53; shepherding is different from individual, 148 ff.

Group-centered leadership, 146, 149

Group dynamics, 143

Group leadership, 143

Group operation: functions necessary for, 149; and negative feelings, 143 ff.